Twenty Five Top CHRISTMAS SONGS

Contents

ISBN 0-7935-2724-4

A Joint Publication of  Music Publisher, New York, New York

and

HAL•LEONARD® CORPORATION

7777 W. BLUEMOUND RD. P.O. BOX 13819 MILWAUKEE, WI 53213

Copyright © 1989 by REGENT MUSIC CORP. and HAL LEONARD PUBLISHING CORPORATION
International Copyright Secured   ALL RIGHTS RESERVED   Printed in the U.S.A.

For all works contained herein:
Unauthorized copying, arranging, adapting, recording or public performance
is an infringement of copyright. Infringers are liable under the law

Visit Hal Leonard online at
www.halleonard.com

PLAYING GUIDE

The songs in this Hal Leonard EASY GUITAR collection are presented with easy-to-read music and lyrics. Chord frames are given to aid the player with left-hand fingerings; however, intermediate and advanced players should feel free to use bar chords or other more advanced chord forms.

These arrangements reflect the style of the original recordings and are presented in easy-to-play keys. You may wish to sing some songs an octave lower than written and/or use a capo to adjust the level to your voice range.

Below the title you will find **strums** and **finger picks** which can be used with each song. See page 3 for an explanation of these symbols.

SAMPLE

FROSTY THE SNOW MAN

Words and Music by STEVE NELSON
and JACK ROLLINS

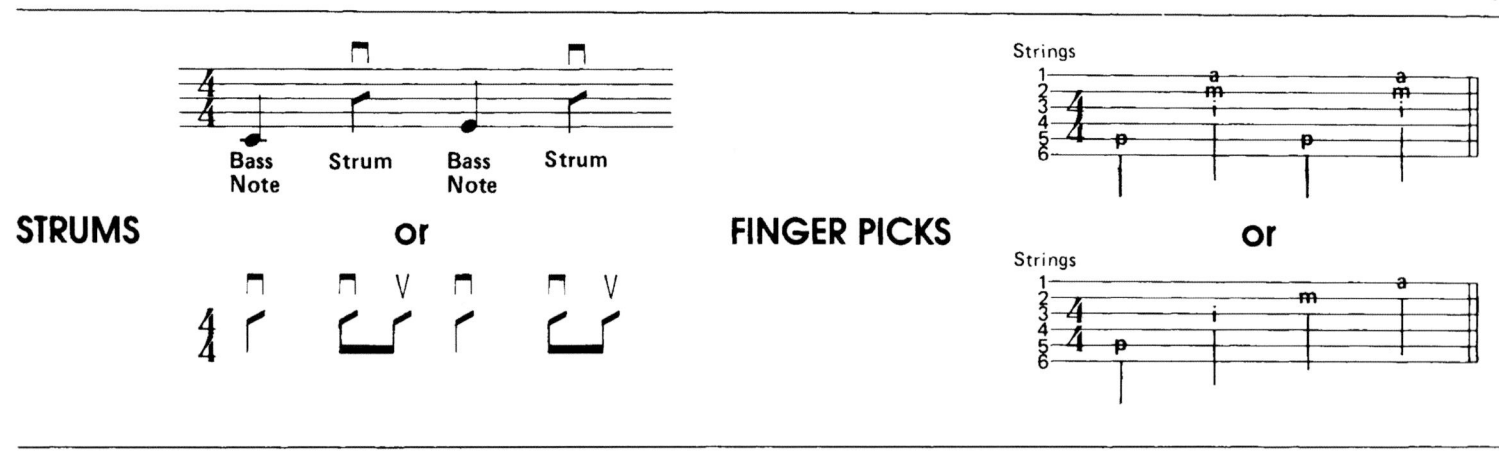

STRUMS   or   **FINGER PICKS**   or

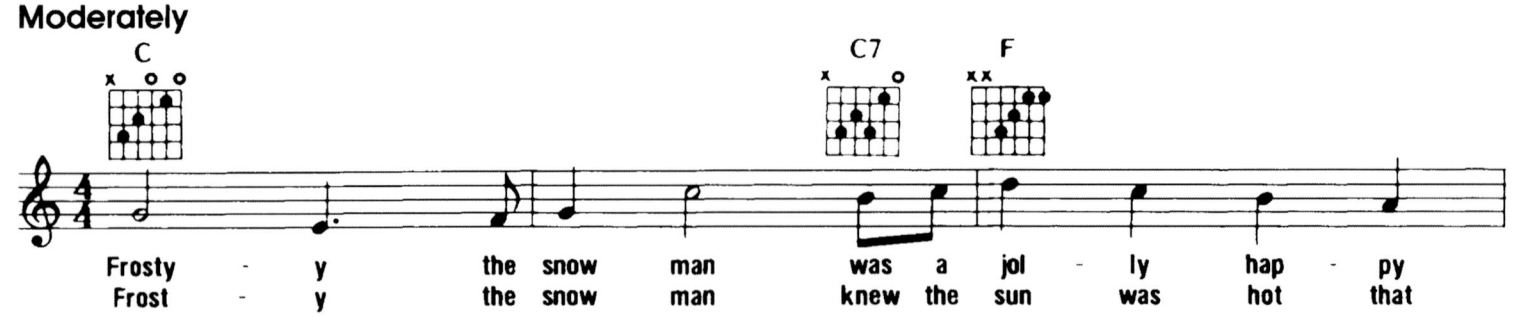

Moderately

Frosty - y the snow man was a jol - ly hap - py
Frost - y the snow man knew the sun was hot that

Copyright © 1950 by Hill & Range Songs, Inc. Copyright Renewed, controlled by Chappell & Co. (Intersong Music, Publisher)
This arrangement Copyright © 1989 by Hill & Range Songs, Inc.
International Copyright Secured   ALL RIGHTS RESERVED   Printed in the U.S.A.
Unauthorized copying, arranging, adapting, recording or public performance is an infringement of copyright.
Infringers are liable under the law.

STRUMS AND FINGER PICKS

Finger picks and strums are written out at the top of each arrangement. The system used throughout all **Hal Leonard Guitar** books is explained below.

FINGER PICKING

The fingers are named p, i, m, a in the following manner:

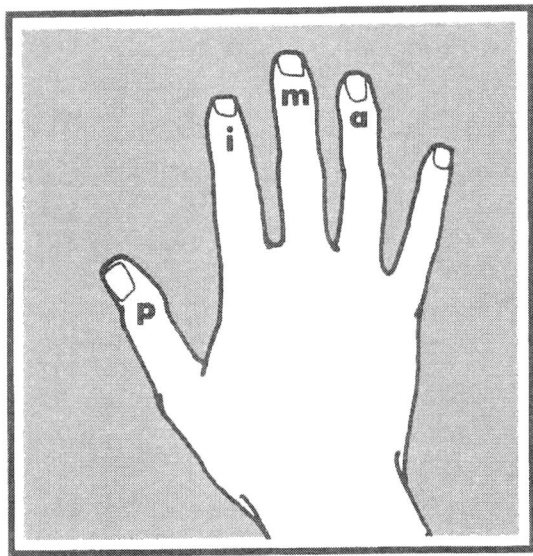

- The thumb (p) plucks strings 4, 5, or 6 depending upon which string is the root of the chord. This motion is a downward stroke. Use the left side of the thumb and thumbnail.
- The other fingers (i, m, a) pluck the string in an upward stroke with the fleshy tip of the finger and fingernail.
- The index finger (i) always plucks string 3.
- The middle finger (m) always plucks string 2.
- The ring finger (a) always plucks string 1.

The thumb and each finger must pluck only one string per stroke and not brush over several strings. (This would be a strum.) Let the strings ring throughout the duration of the chord.

Strums

The Strum symbols and their meanings are as follows:

     ⊓ — Down stroke
     V — Up stroke
     X — Dampening with the hand

BLUE CHRISTMAS

Words and Music by BILLY HAYES
and JAY JOHNSON

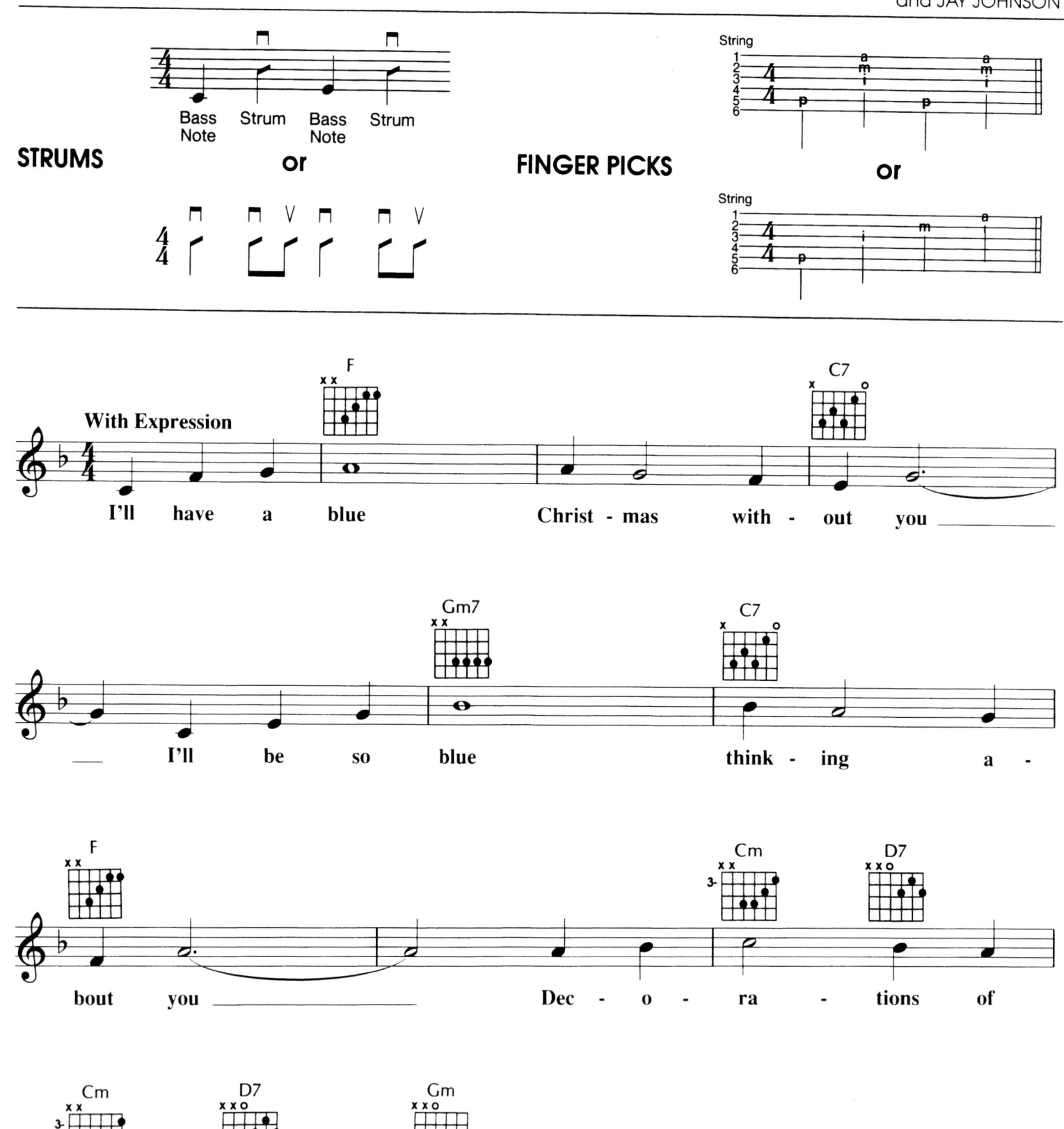

Copyright © 1948 PolyGram International Publishing, Inc.
Copyright Renewed
This arrangement Copyright © 1989 PolyGram International Publishing, Inc.
International Copyright Secured   All Rights Reserved

Won't mean a thing if you're not here with me, I'll have a

blue Christ - mas, that's cer - tain

And when that blue heart - ache starts hurt - in'

You'll be do - in' all right, with your

Christ - mas of white, But I'll have a

blue, blue Christ - mas.

CARRYING THE LORD TO JERUSALEM
(Little White Donkey)

By ROY C. BENNETT

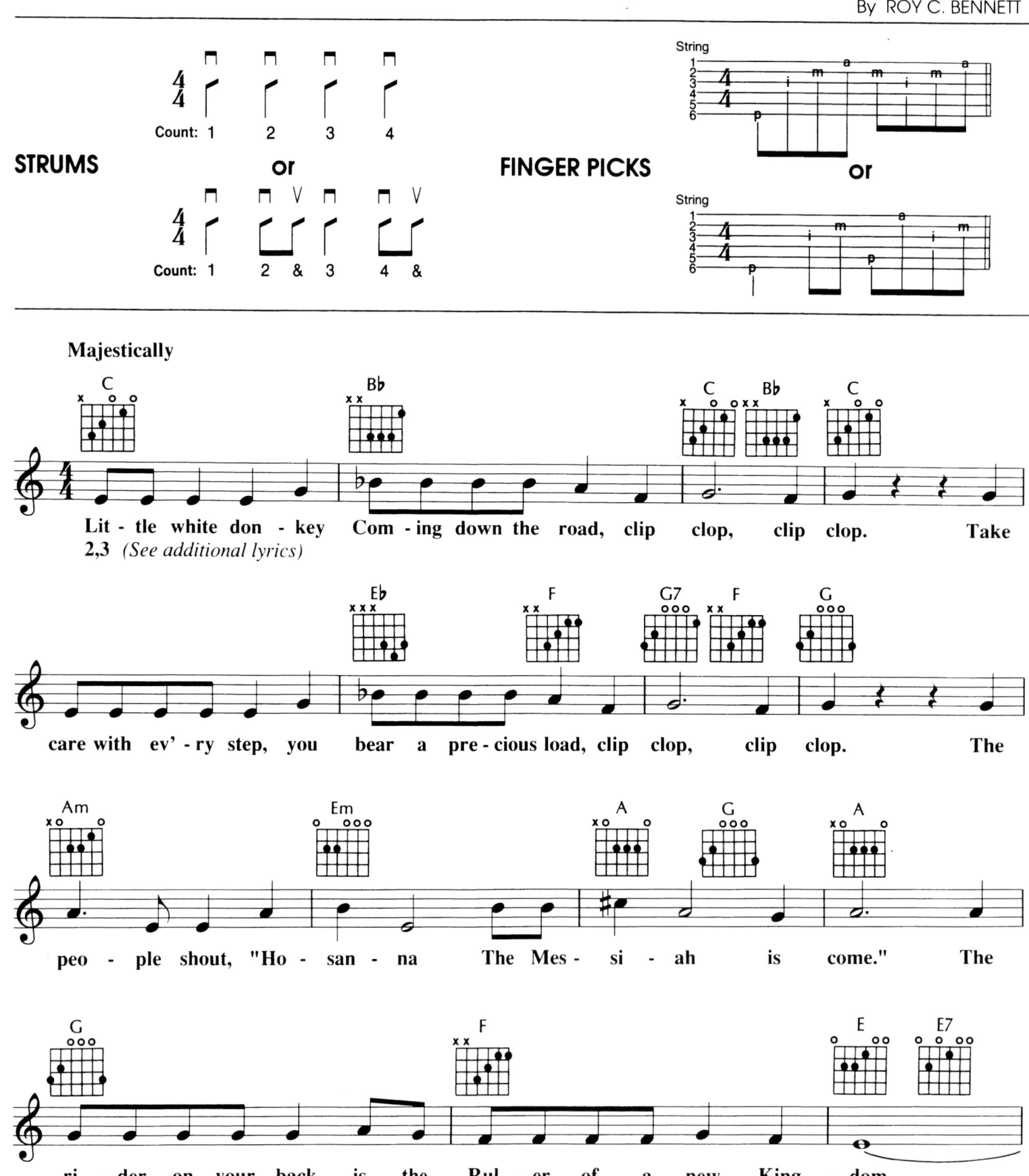

Copyright © 1969, 1989 by Jewel Music Publishing Co., Inc.
All Rights Reserved.

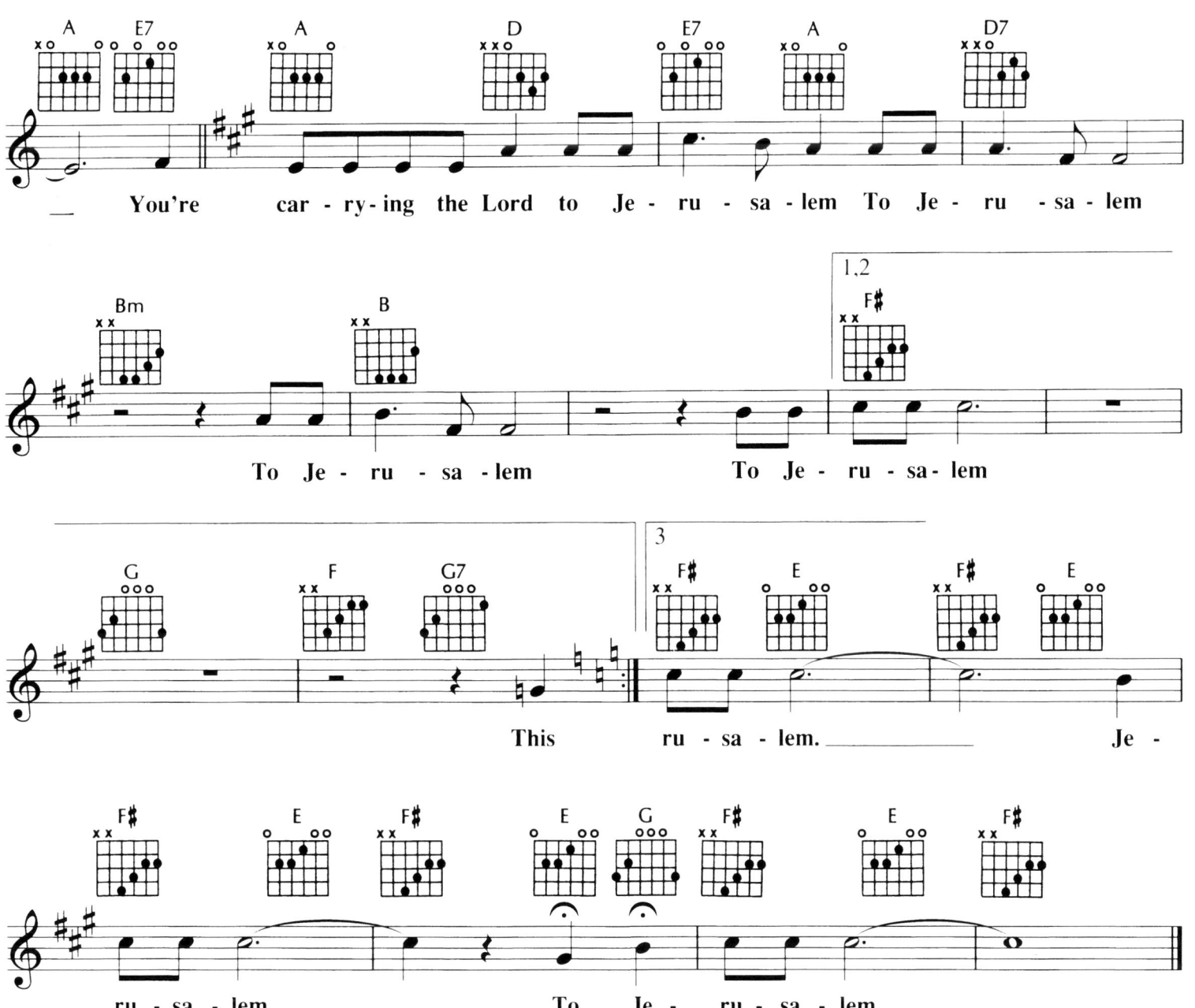

You're car-ry-ing the Lord to Je - ru - sa - lem   To Je - ru - sa - lem

To Je - ru - sa - lem   To Je - ru - sa - lem

This   ru - sa - lem. _____   Je -

ru - sa - lem. _____   To Je - ru - sa - lem. _____

2. Shepherd of mankind has a mission to fulfill.
   He must show His flock the path to peace and goodwill.
   The people spread their garments to smoothen your way.
   You're thirsty and you're, but you mustn't falter once today.

   Chorus

3. Little white donkey when your blessed journey's through,
   Clip, clop.
   Though you're just a donkey all men will be blessing you,
   Clip, clop.
   For you're the one He's chosen in all Galilee.
   Lift up your head and be proud of your destiny.

   Chorus

THE CHRISTMAS WALTZ

Lyric by SAMMY CAHN
Music by JULE STYNE

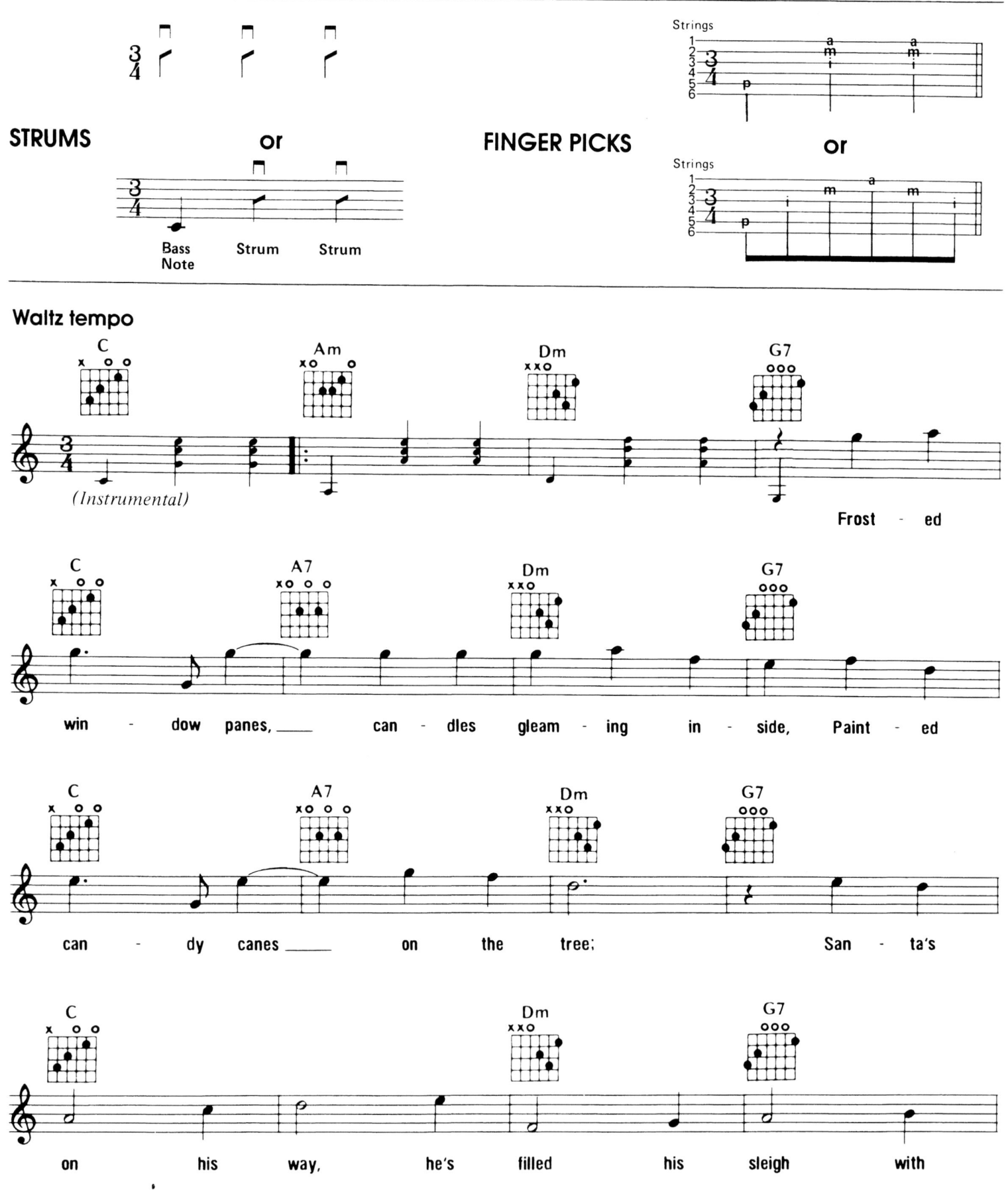

Copyright © 1954 by Sands Music. Copyright Renewed, assigned to Producers Music, Inc. (Chappell & Co., Administrator) and Cahn Music, Inc.
This arrangement Copyright © 1989 by Producers Music, Inc. and Cahn Music, Inc.
International Copyright Secured   ALL RIGHTS RESERVED   Printed in the U.S.A.
Unauthorized copying, arranging, adapting, recording or public performance is an infringement of copyright
Infringers are liable under the law.

C*H*R*I*S*T*M*A*S

By JACK FULTON
and LOIS STEELE

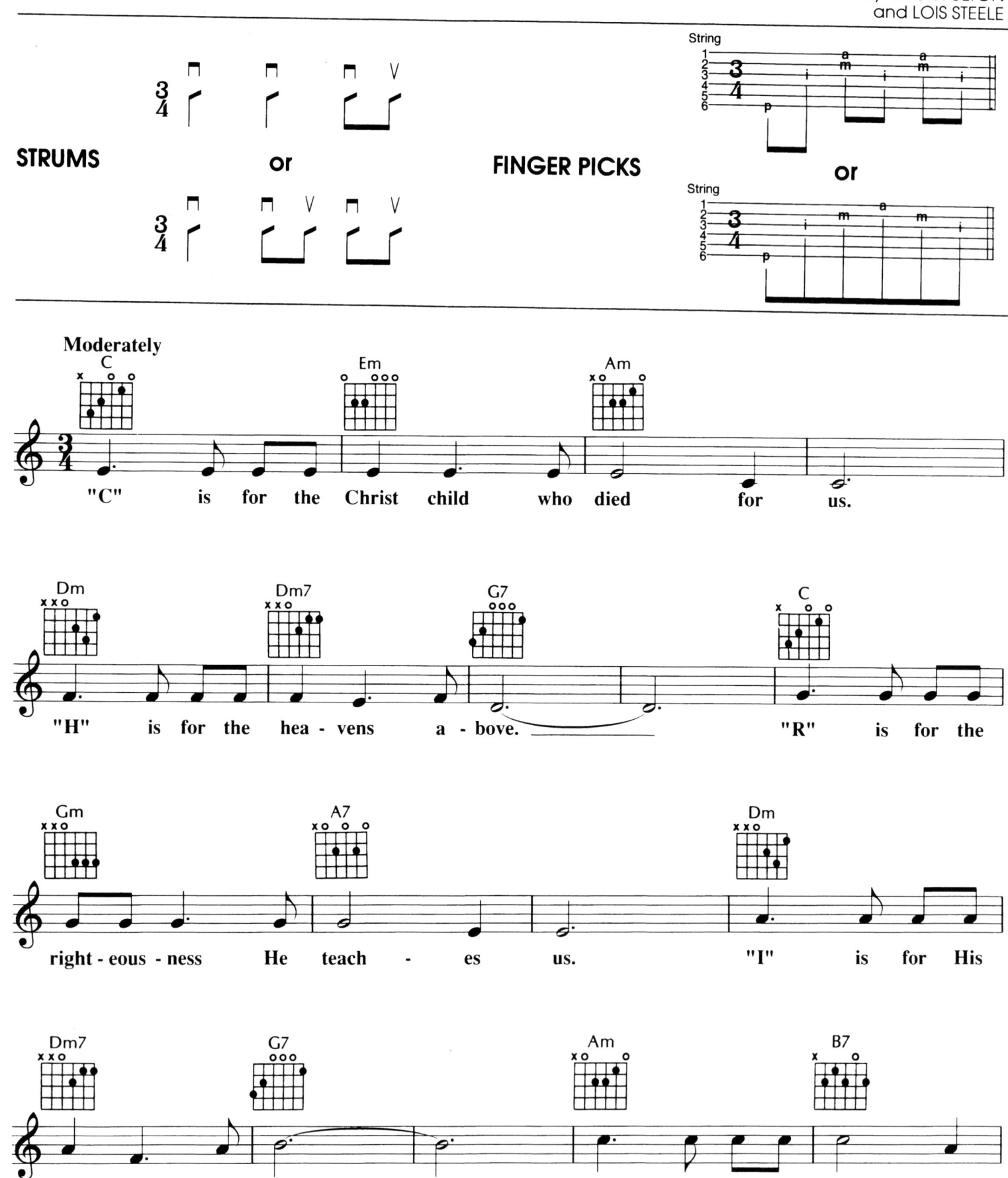

Copyright © 1961, 1989 (Renewed) by Jewel Music Publishing Co., Inc.
All Rights Reserved.

DO YOU HEAR WHAT I HEAR

By NOEL REGNEY
and GLORIA SHAYNE

Count: 1 2 3 4

STRUMS or **FINGER PICKS** or

Count: 1 (& 2) & 3 4 &

Like a March

1. Said the night wind to the lit - tle lamb, Do you see what I see!
2,3. *(See additional lyrics)*

Way up in the sky, lit - tle lamb, Do you see what I see?

A star, a star Danc - ing in the night, with a

tail as big as a kite, With a tail as big as a

Copyright © 1962, 1989 by Regent Music Corp.
All Rights Reserved

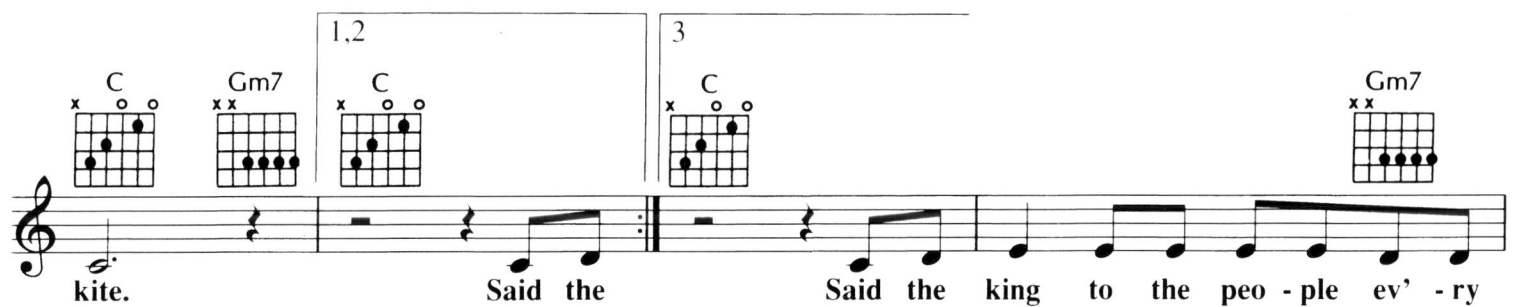

kite. Said the Said the king to the peo - ple ev' - ry

where Lis - ten to what I say! ____ Pray for peace, peo - ple ev' - ry

where Lis - ten to what I say! ____ The Child The Child,

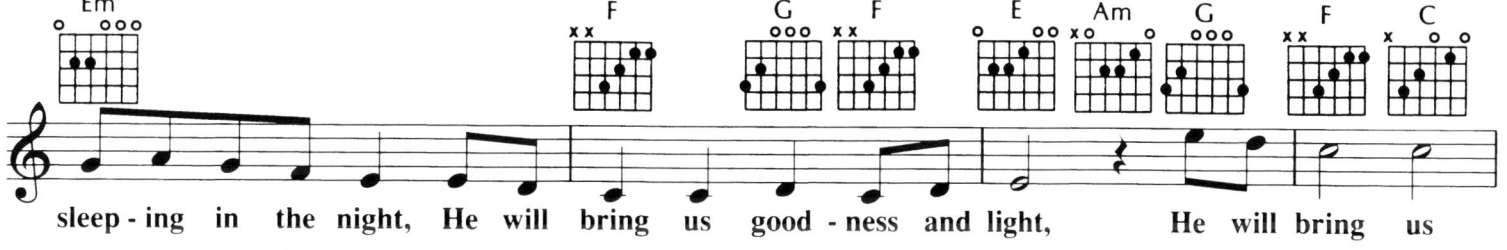

sleep - ing in the night, He will bring us good - ness and light, He will bring us

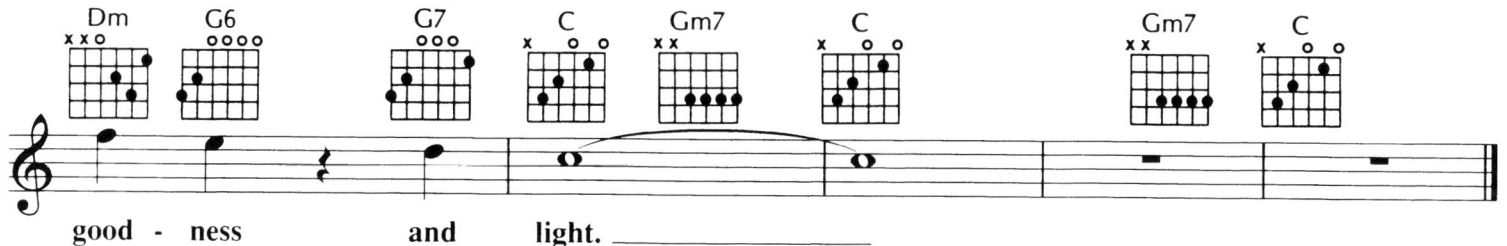

good - ness and light. _____

Additional Lyrics

2. (Said the) little lamb to the shepherd boy.
   Do you hear what I hear?
   Ringing in the sky, shepherd boy,
   Do you hear what I hear?
   A song, a song high above the tree,
   With a voice as big as the sea.

3. (Said the) shepherd boy to the mighty king,
   Do you know what I know?
   In your palace warm, mighty king,
   Do you know what I know?
   A child, a child shivers in the cold;
   Let us bring him silver and gold
   Let us bring him silver and gold.

FROSTY THE SNOW MAN

Words and Music by STEVE NELSON
and JACK ROLLINS

Copyright © 1950 by Hill & Range Songs, Inc. Copyright Renewed, controlled by Chappell & Co. (Intersong Music, Publisher)
This arrangement Copyright © 1989 by Hill & Range Songs, Inc.
International Copyright Secured   ALL RIGHTS RESERVED   Printed in the U.S.A.
Unauthorized copying, arranging, adapting, recording or public performance is an infringement of copyright.
Infringers are liable under the law.

14

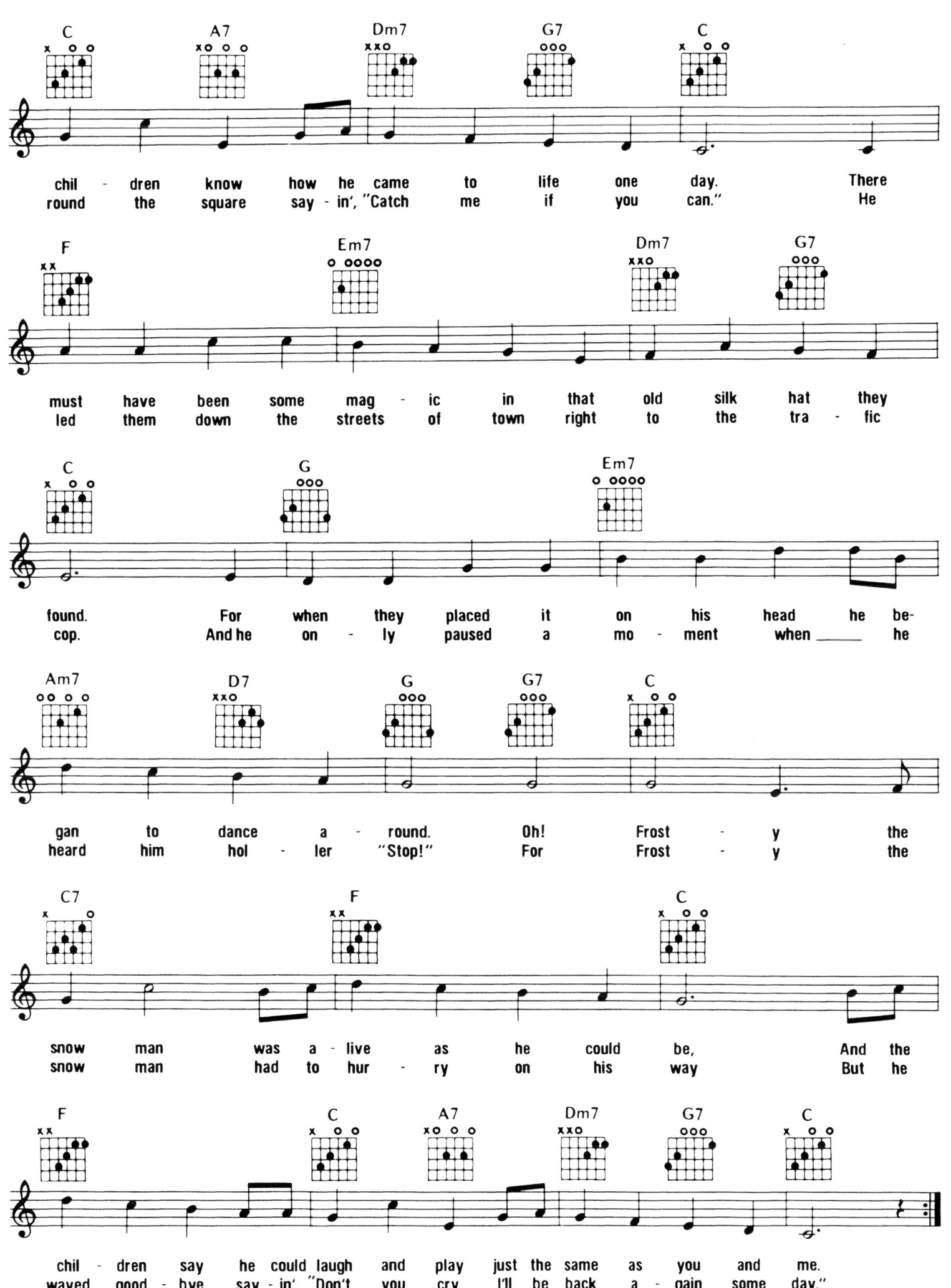

HAVE YOURSELF A MERRY LITTLE CHRISTMAS

By HUGH MARTIN
and RALPH BLANE

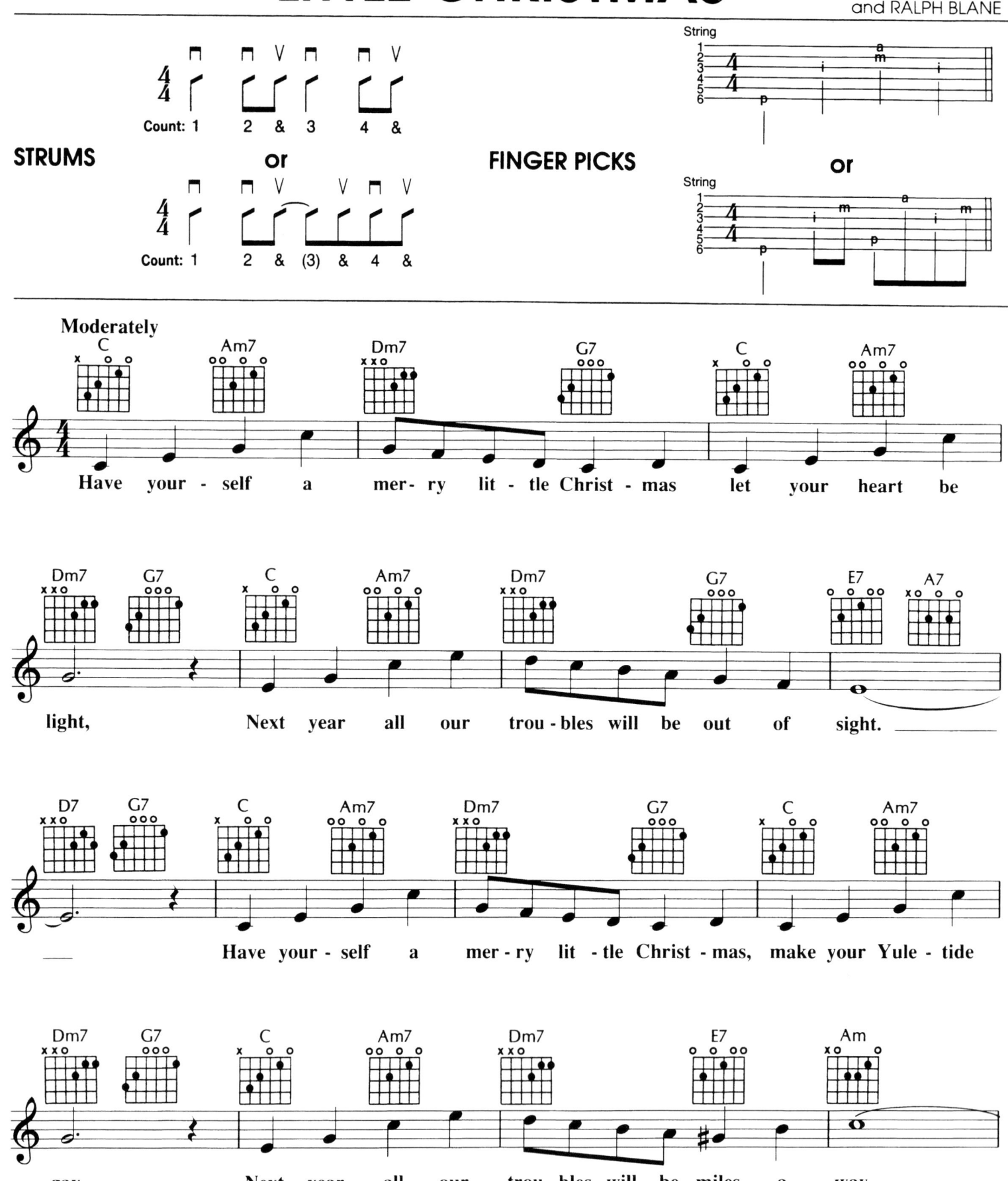

STRUMS   or   FINGER PICKS   or

Count: 1 2 & 3 4 &

Count: 1 2 & (3) & 4 &

Moderately

Have your-self a mer-ry lit-tle Christ-mas let your heart be

light, Next year all our trou-bles will be out of sight. _____

_____ Have your-self a mer-ry lit-tle Christ-mas, make your Yule-tide

gay, Next year all our trou-bles will be miles a-way. _____

Copyright © 1943 (Renewed 1971) Metro-Goldwyn Mayer, Inc.
Copyright © 1944 (Renewed 1972) Leo Feist, Inc.
This arrangement Copyright © 1980 Leo Feist, Inc.
All Rights to Leo Feist, Inc. assigned to SBK Catalogue Partnership
All Rights Controlled and Administered by SBK Catalogue
International Copyright Secured   Made in U.S.A.   All Rights Reserved

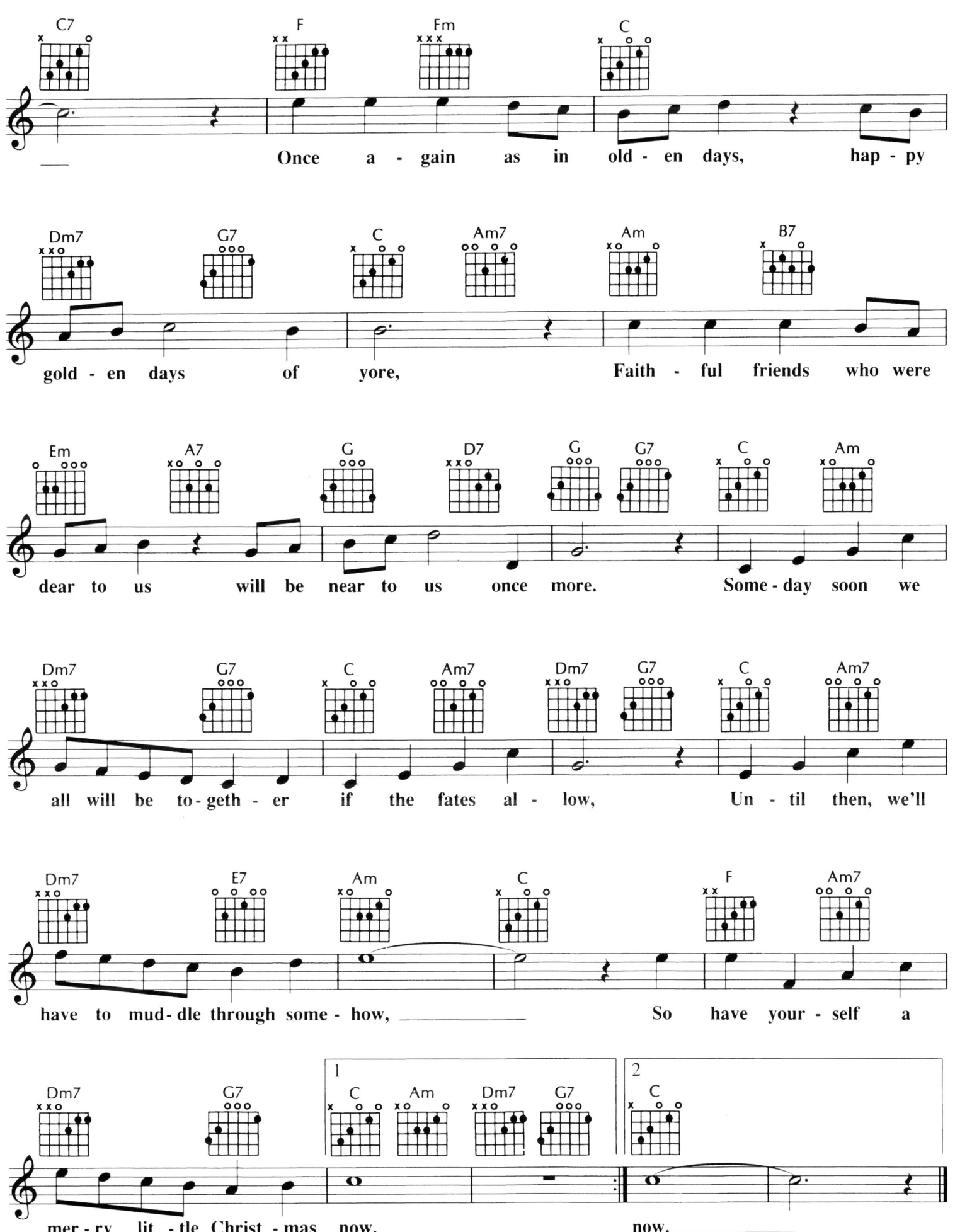

Once a - gain as in old - en days, hap - py

gold - en days of yore, Faith - ful friends who were

dear to us will be near to us once more. Some - day soon we

all will be to - geth - er if the fates al - low, Un - til then, we'll

have to mud - dle through some - how, _____ So have your - self a

mer - ry lit - tle Christ - mas now. now. _____

HERE COMES SANTA CLAUS

By GENE AUTRY
and OAKLEY HALDMAN

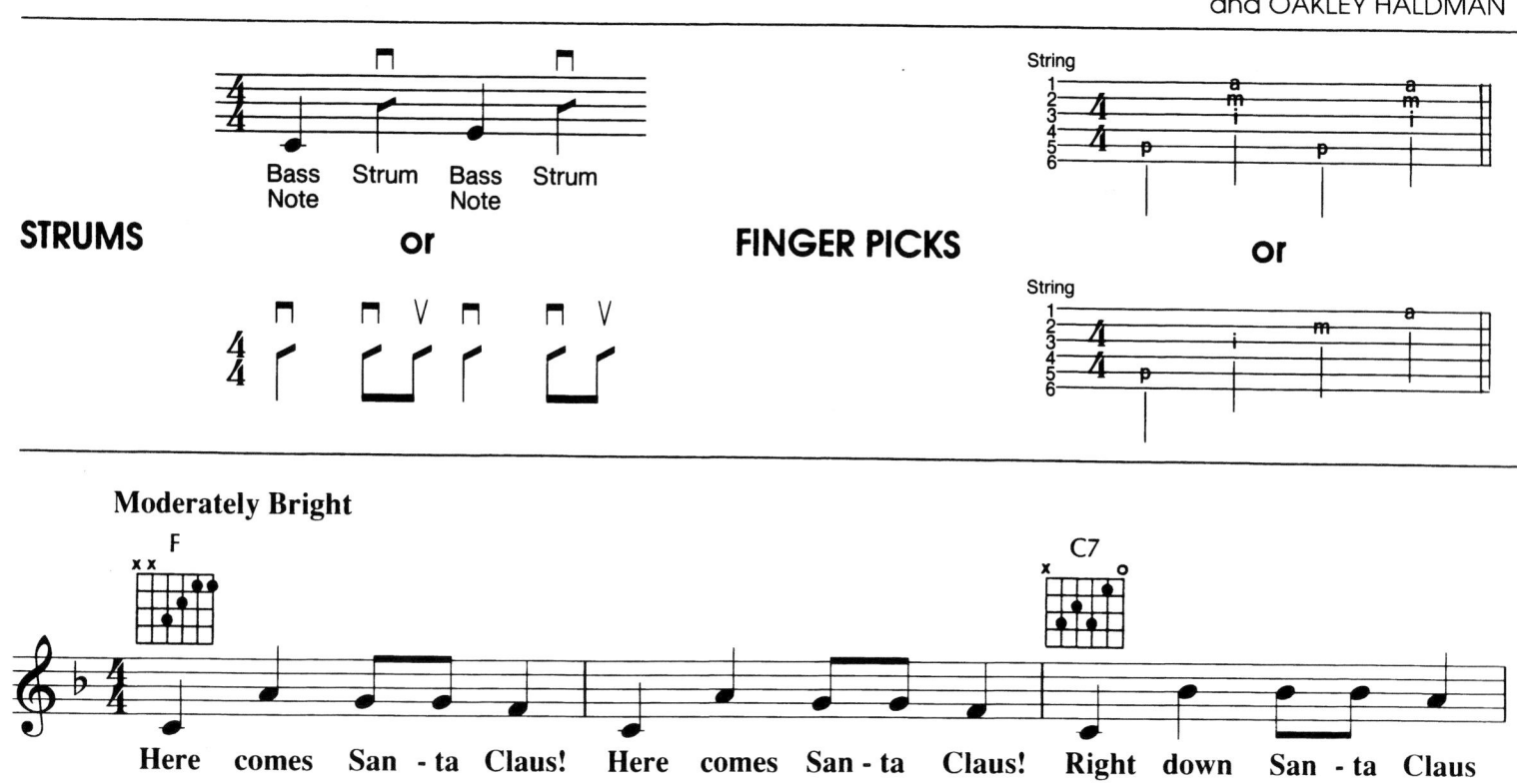

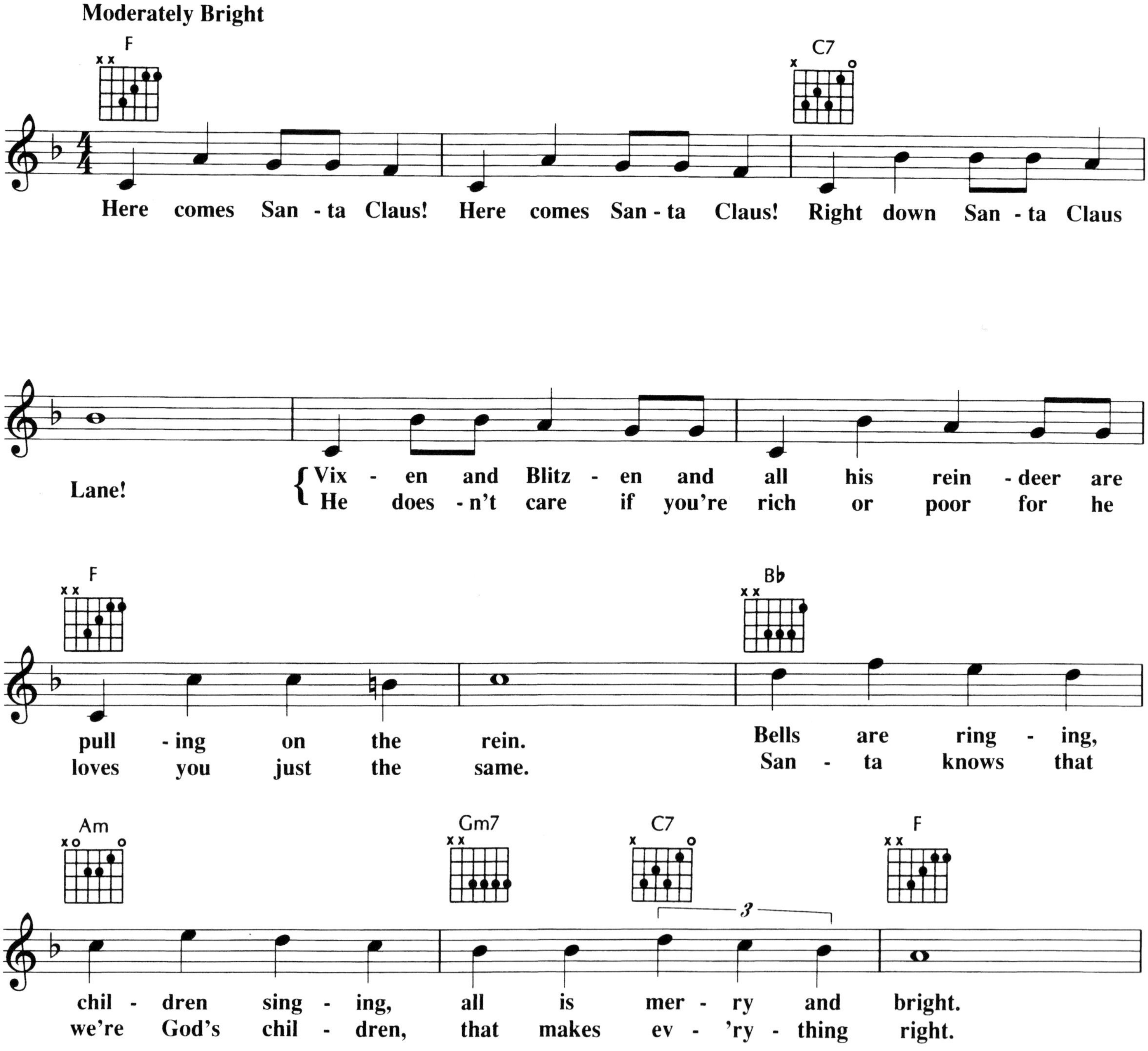

STRUMS or **FINGER PICKS** or

Bass Note · Strum · Bass Note · Strum

Moderately Bright

F   C7

Here comes San - ta Claus! Here comes San - ta Claus! Right down San - ta Claus

Lane!

{ Vix - en and Blitz - en and all his rein - deer are
He does - n't care if you're rich or poor for he

F   Bb

pull - ing on the rein.   Bells are ring - ing,
loves you just the same.   San - ta knows that

Am   Gm7   C7   F

3

chil - dren sing - ing, all is mer - ry and bright.
we're God's chil - dren, that makes ev - 'ry - thing right.

Copyright © 1946, 1989 (Renewed) Western Publishing Co.
International Copyright Secured   Made in U.S.A.   All Rights Reserved

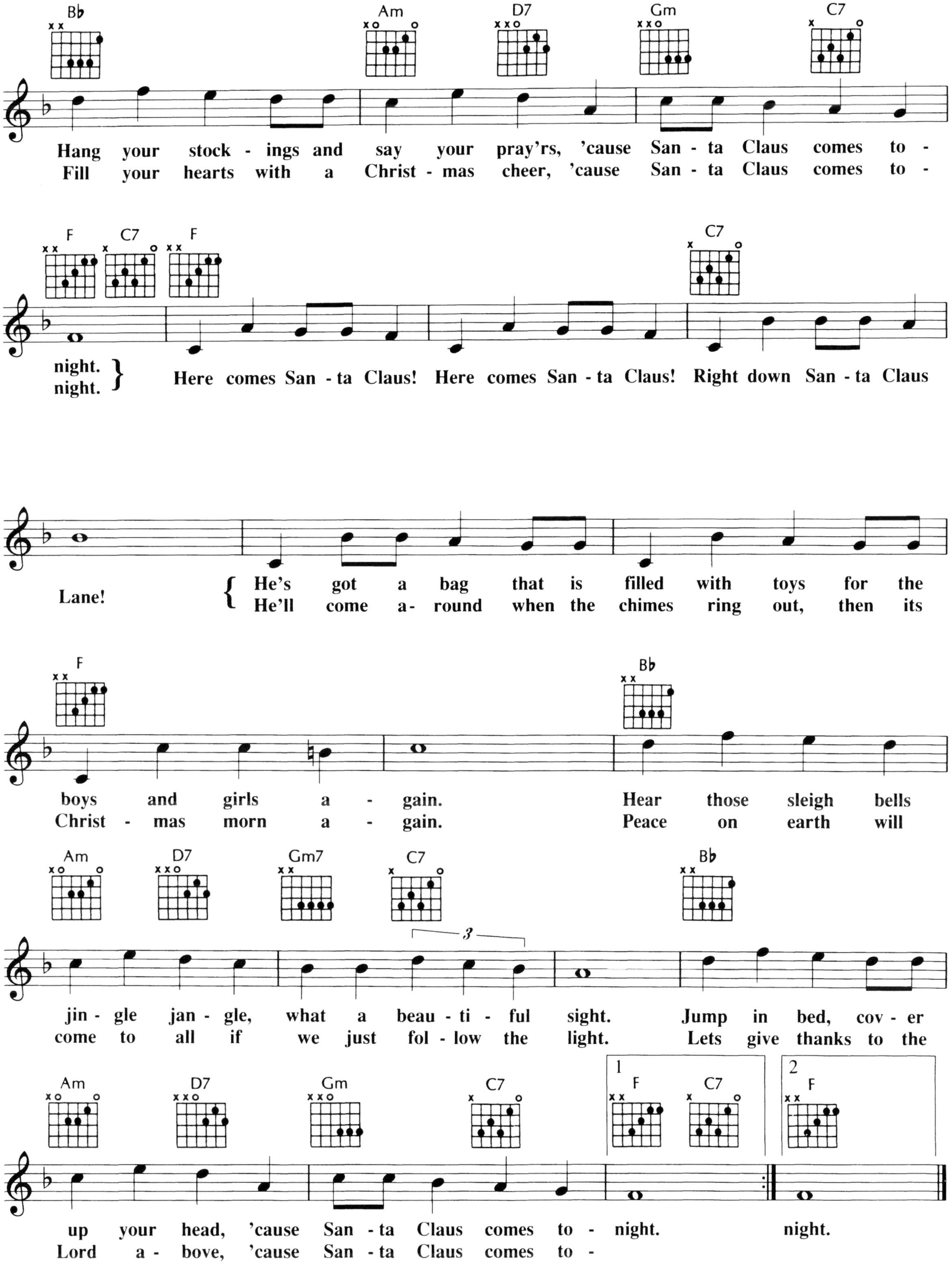
Bb Am D7 Gm C7
Hang your stock - ings and say your pray'rs, 'cause San - ta Claus comes to -
Fill your hearts with a Christ - mas cheer, 'cause San - ta Claus comes to -
F C7 F C7
night. night. Here comes San - ta Claus! Here comes San - ta Claus! Right down San - ta Claus
Lane! He's got a bag that is filled with toys for the
He'll come a- round when the chimes ring out, then its
F Bb
boys and girls a - gain. Hear those sleigh bells
Christ - mas morn a - gain. Peace on earth will
Am D7 Gm7 C7 Bb
3
jin - gle jan - gle, what a beau - ti - ful sight. Jump in bed, cov - er
come to all if we just fol - low the light. Lets give thanks to the
Am D7 Gm C7 1 F C7 2 F
up your head, 'cause San - ta Claus comes to - night. night.
Lord a - bove, 'cause San - ta Claus comes to -

A HOLLY JOLLY CHRISTMAS

Words and Music by
JOHNNY MARKS

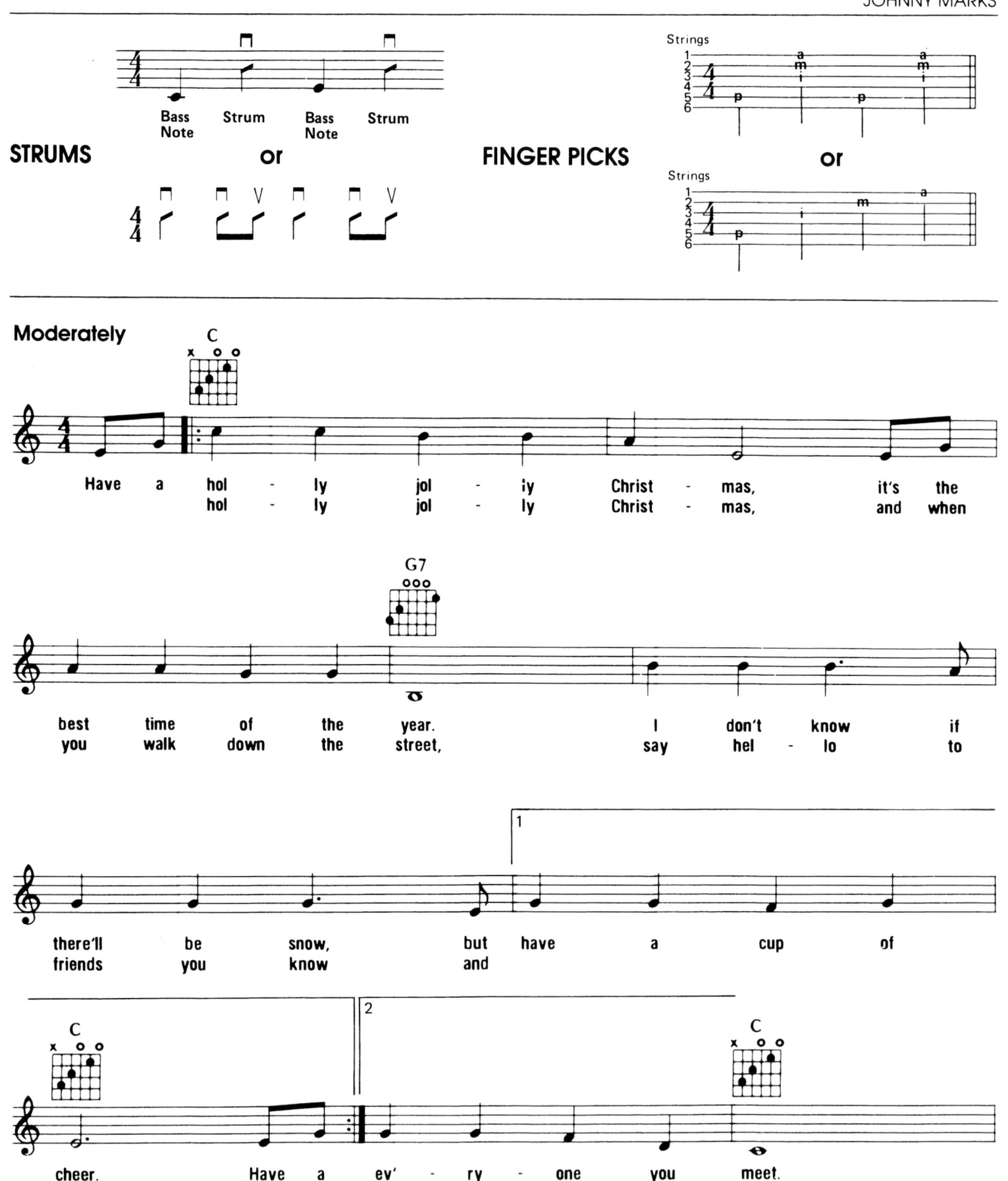

Copyright © 1962 & 1964 by St. Nicholas Music, Inc., 1619 Broadway, New York, New York 10019
This arrangement Copyright © 1989 by St. Nicholas Music, Inc.
All Rights Reserved

(There's No Place Like)
HOME FOR THE HOLIDAYS

Words by AL STILLMAN
Music by ROBERT ALLEN

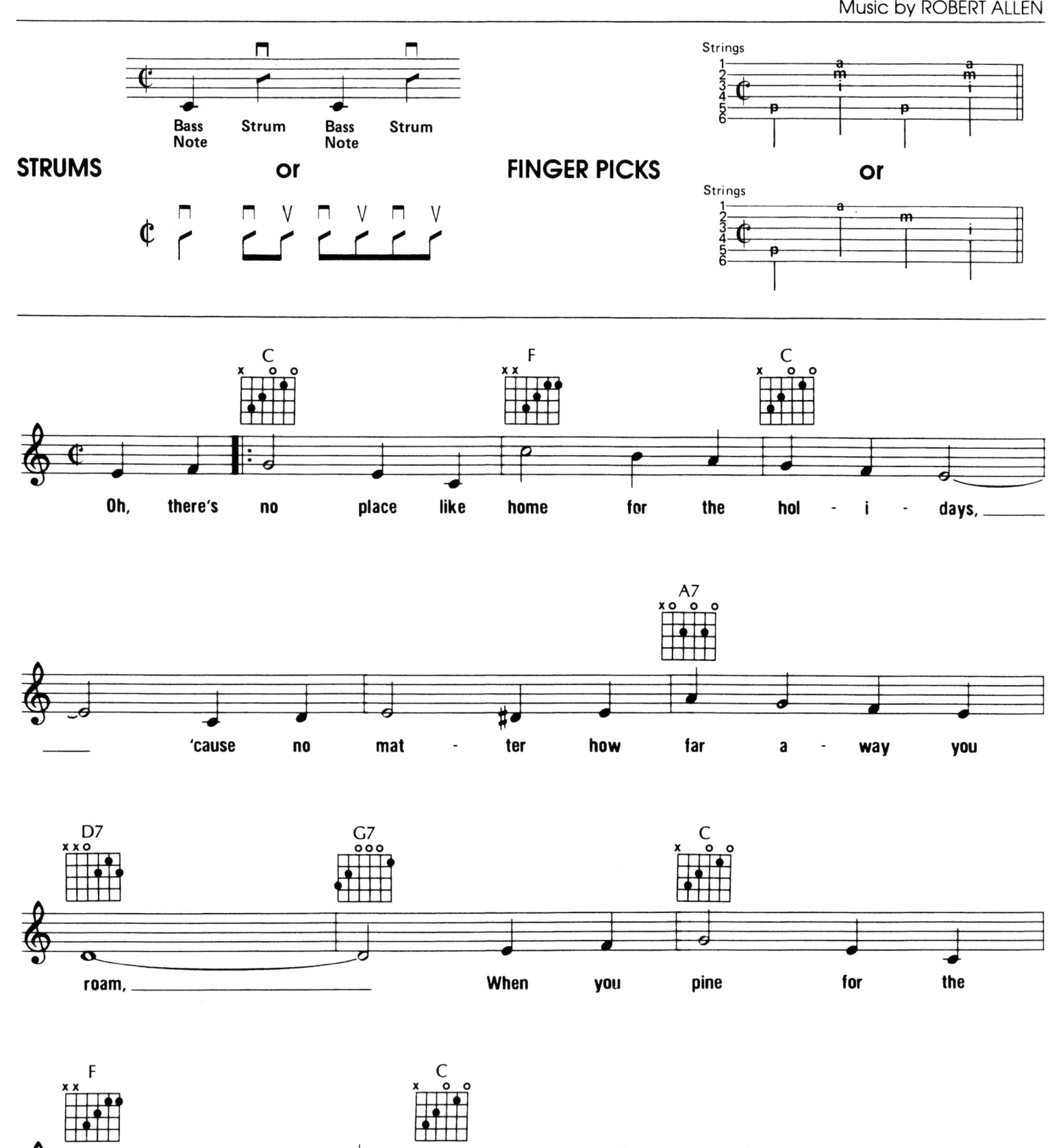

© Copyright 1954 Roncom Music Co. Copyright Renewed 1982.
Renewed Copyright Assigned to Charlie Deitcher Productions, Inc. and Kitty Anne Music Co.
This arrangement Copyright © 1989 Charlie Deitcher Productions, Inc. and Kitty Anne Music Co.
International Copyright Secured   Made in U.S.A.   All Rights Reserved

hol - i - days you can't beat home sweet home.

I met a man who lives in Ten - nes - see and

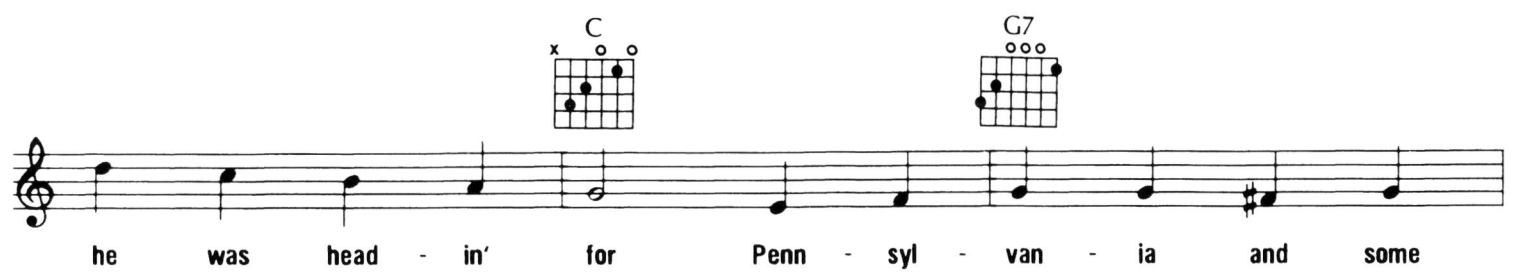

he was head - in' for Penn - syl - van - ia and some

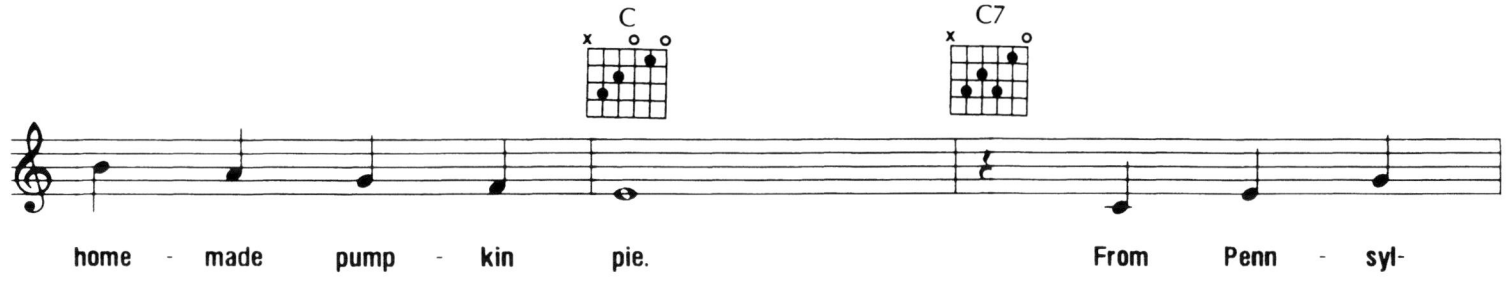

home - made pump - kin pie. From Penn - syl-

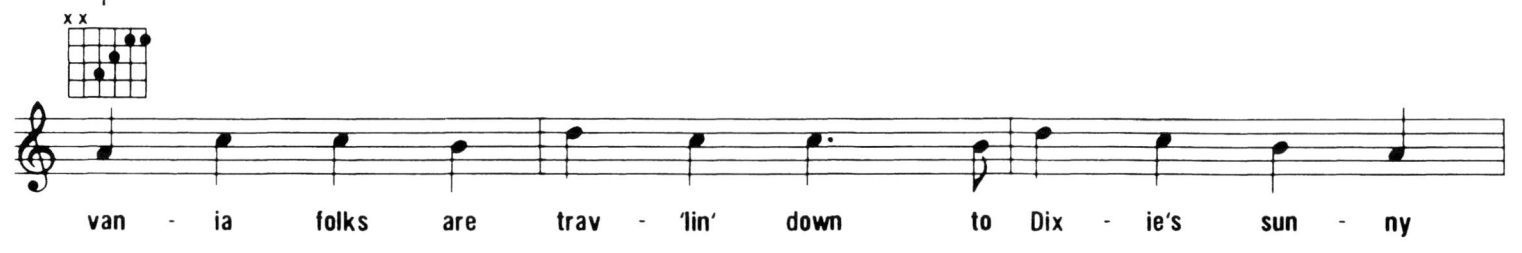

van - ia folks are trav - 'lin' down to Dix - ie's sun - ny

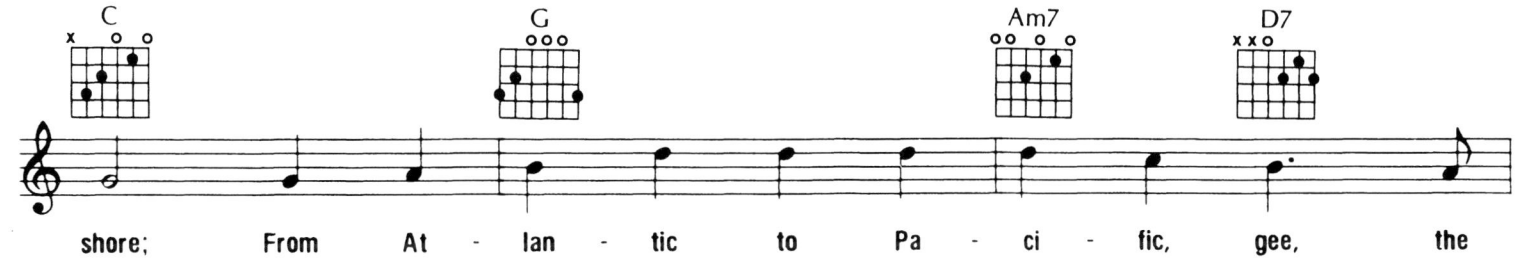

shore; From At - lan - tic to Pa - ci - fic, gee, the

JINGLE-BELL ROCK

Words and Music by JOE BEAL
and JIM BOOTHE

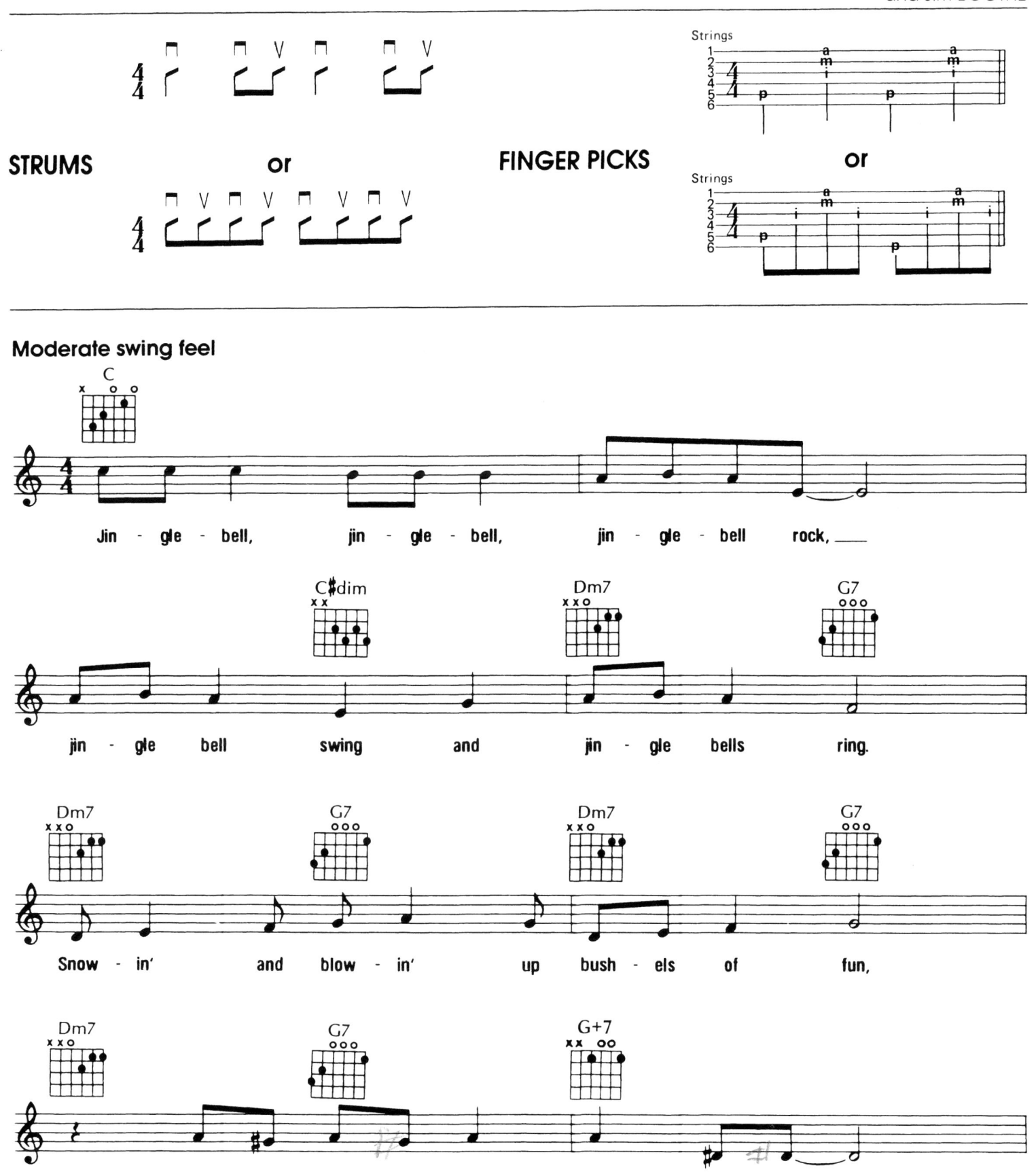

STRUMS   or   **FINGER PICKS**   or

Moderate swing feel

Jin - gle - bell,   jin - gle - bell,   jin - gle - bell rock, ___

jin - gle bell swing   and   jin - gle bells ring.

Snow - in'   and   blow - in'   up   bush - els of   fun,

now   the   jin - gle hop   has   be - gun. ___

Copyright © 1957 by Cornell Music, Inc.
All Rights controlled by Chappell & Co. (Intersong Music, Publisher)
This arrangement Copyright © 1989 by Chappell & Co.
International Copyright Secured   ALL RIGHTS RESERVED   Printed in the U.S.A.
Unauthorized copying, arranging, adapting, recording or public performance is an infringement of copyright.
Infringers are liable under the law.

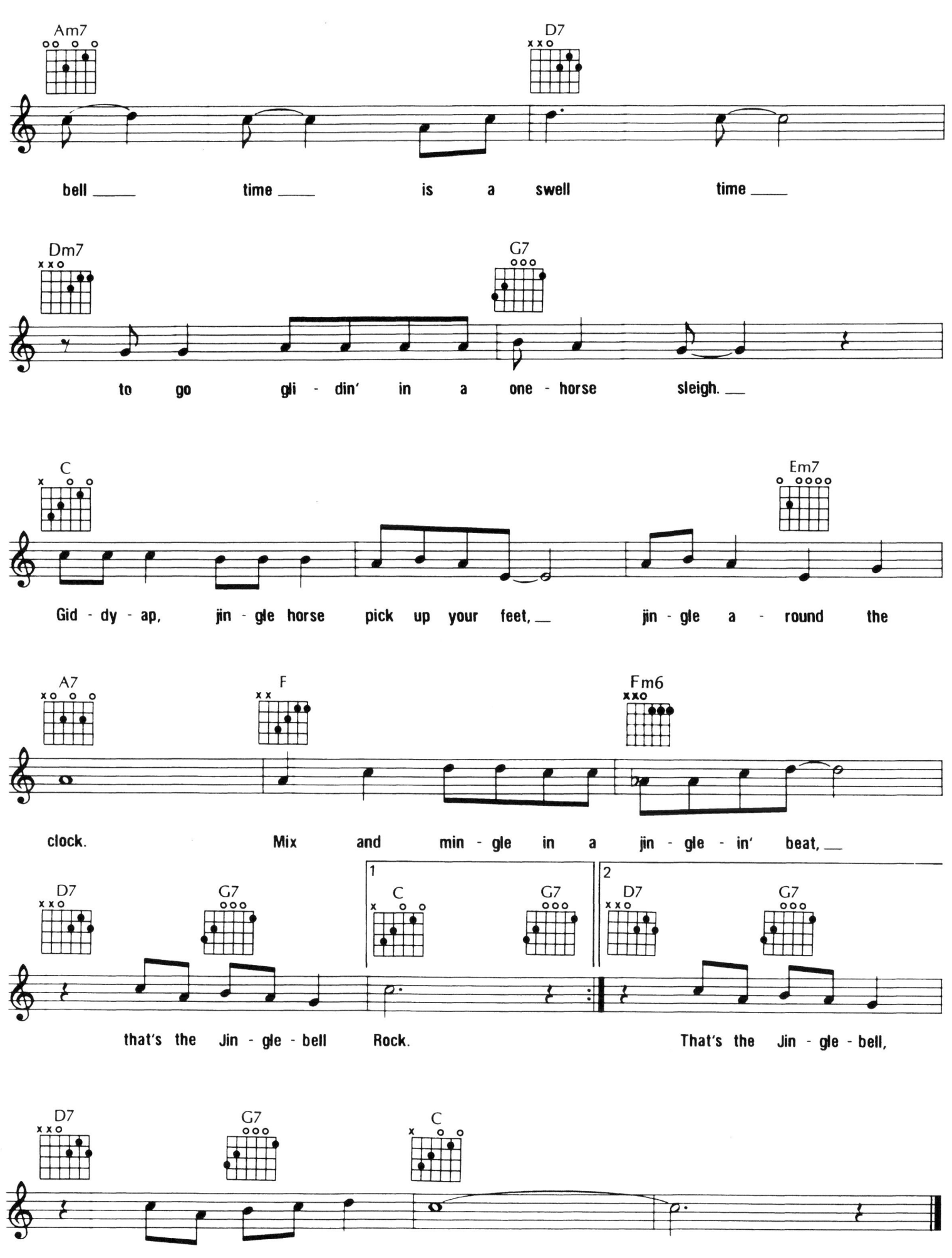

bell _____ time _____ is a swell time _____

to go gli - din' in a one - horse sleigh. __

Gid - dy - ap, jin - gle horse pick up your feet, __ jin - gle a - round the

clock. Mix and min - gle in a jin - gle - in' beat, __

1.
that's the Jin - gle - bell Rock.

2.
That's the Jin - gle - bell,

That's the Jin - gle - bell Rock. _____

27

I SAW MOMMY KISSING SANTA CLAUS

Words and Music by
TOMMIE CONNOR

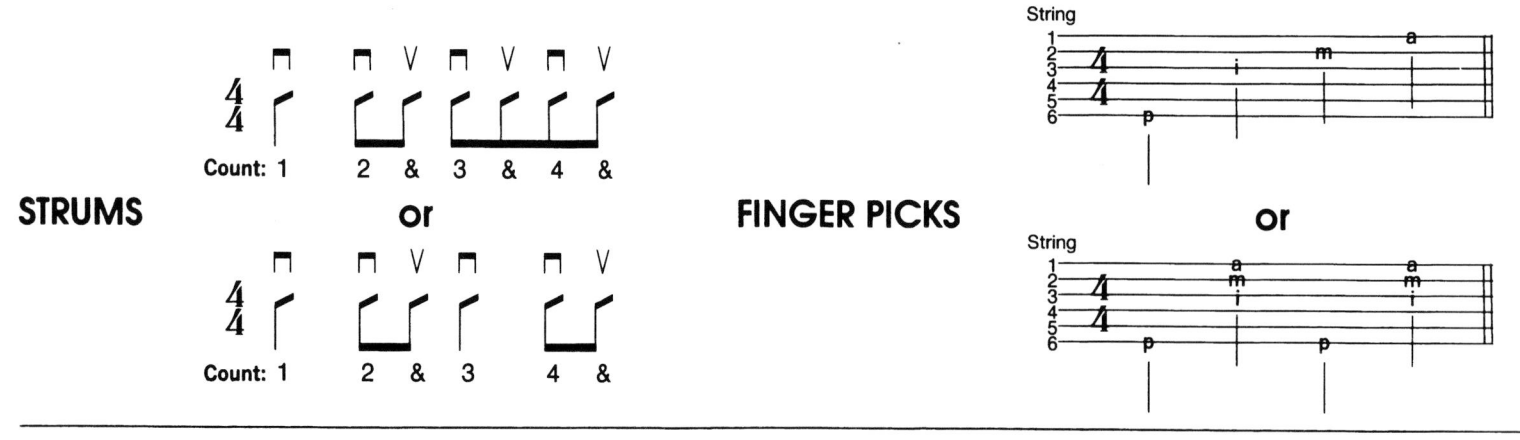

STRUMS or FINGER PICKS or

Moderately

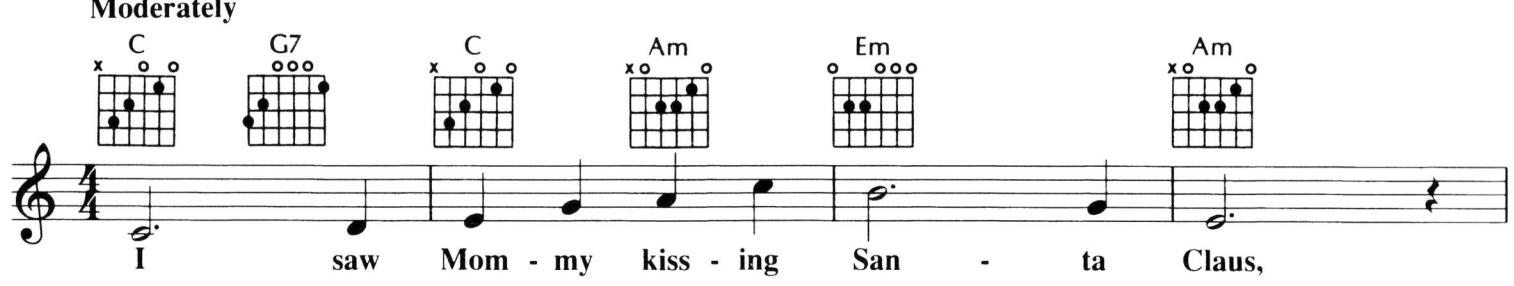

I saw Mom - my kiss - ing San - ta Claus,

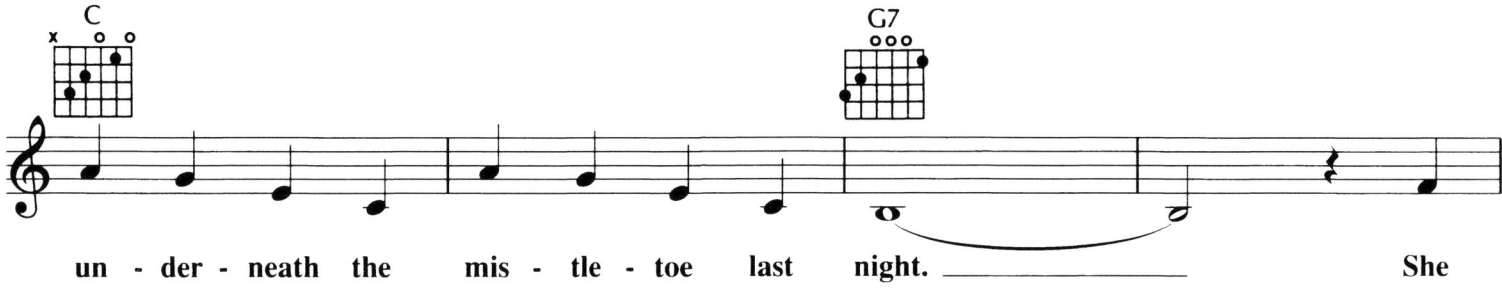

un - der - neath the mis - tle - toe last night. _____ She

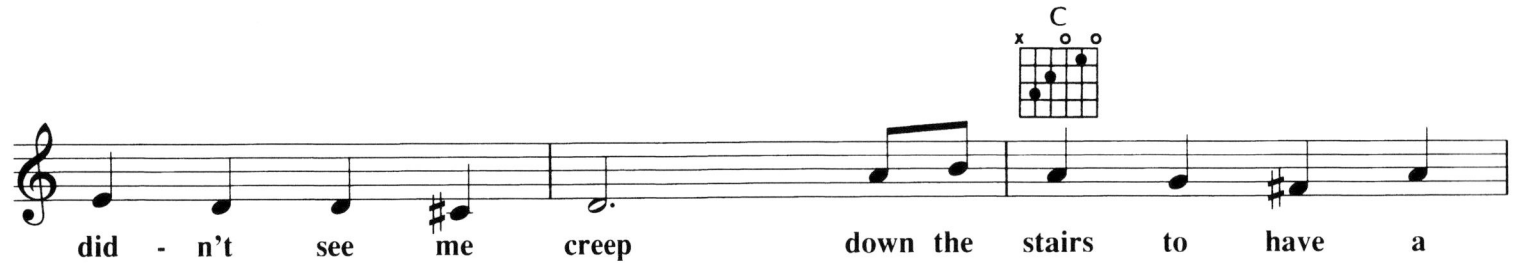

did - n't see me creep down the stairs to have a

peep, she thought that I was tucked up in my

Copyright © 1952 (Renewed) Jewel Music Publishing Co., Inc.
This arrangement Copyright © 1989 Jewel Music Publishing Co., Inc.
All Rights Reserved

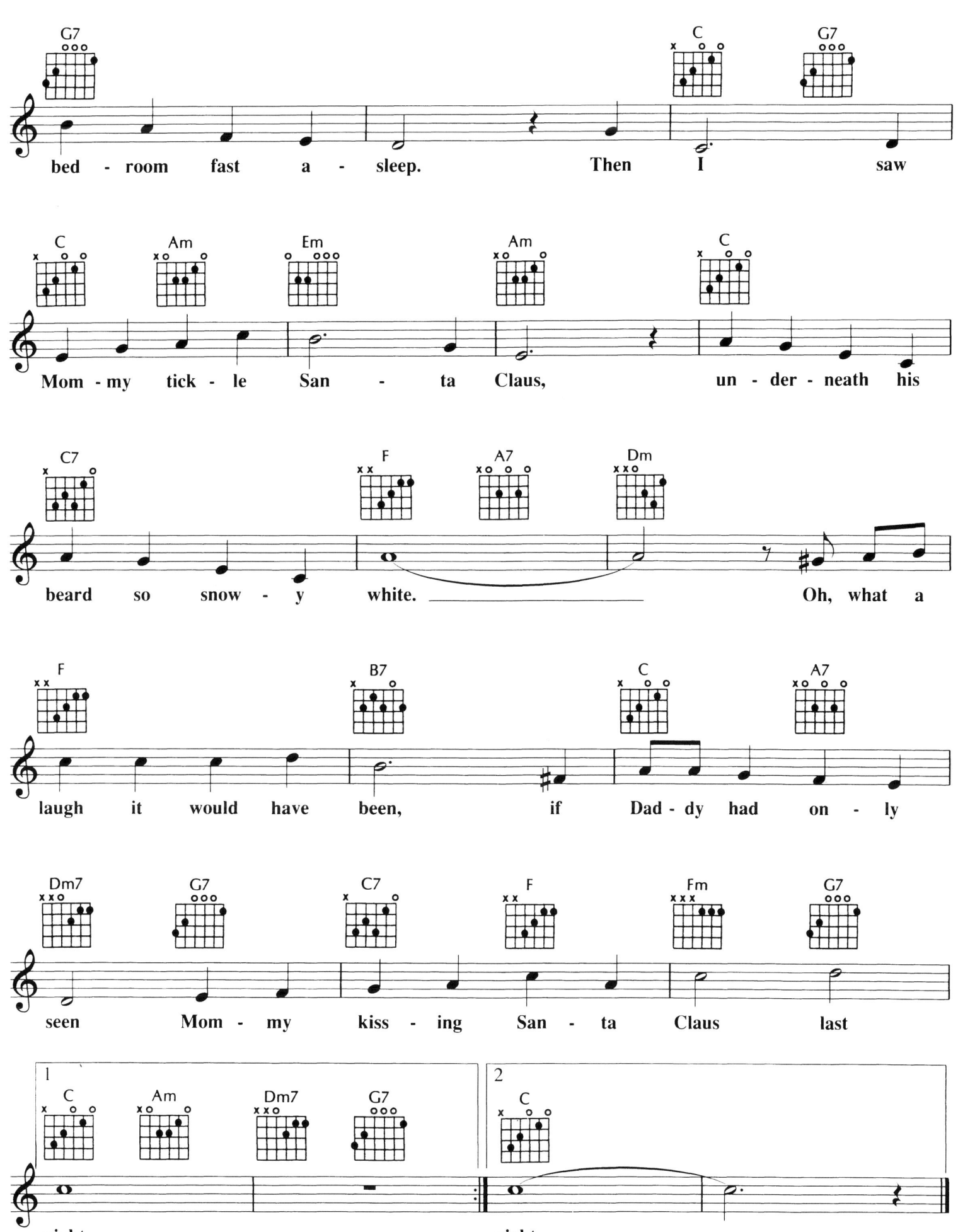

I'LL BE HOME FOR CHRISTMAS

Words and Music by KIM GANNON
and WALTER KENT

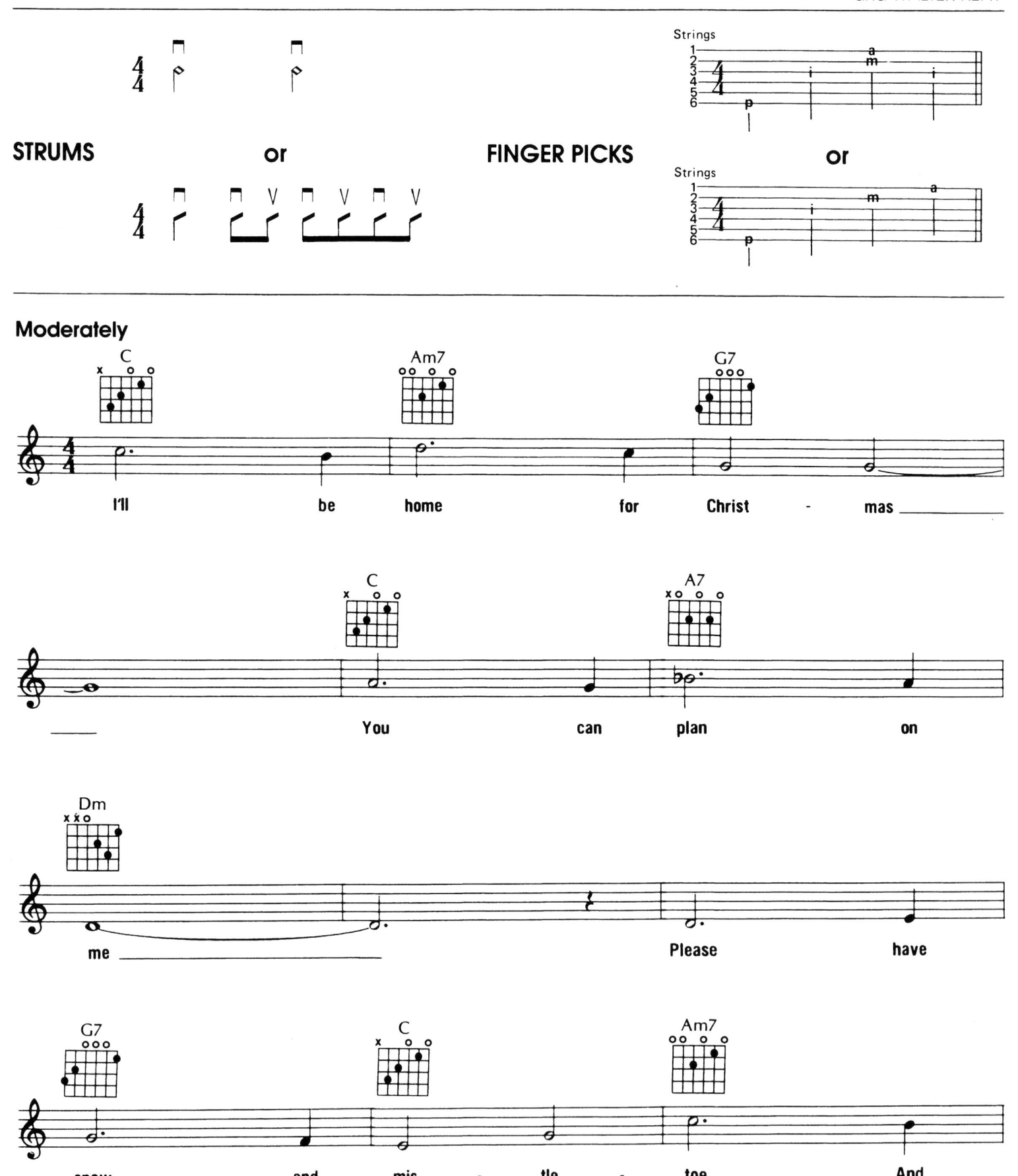

© Copyright 1943 by Gannon & Kent Music Co., Inc. Beverly Hills, CA
Copyright Renewed
This arrangement Copyright © 1989 by Gannon & Kent Music Co., Inc.
International Copyright Secured   Made in U.S.A.   All Rights Reserved

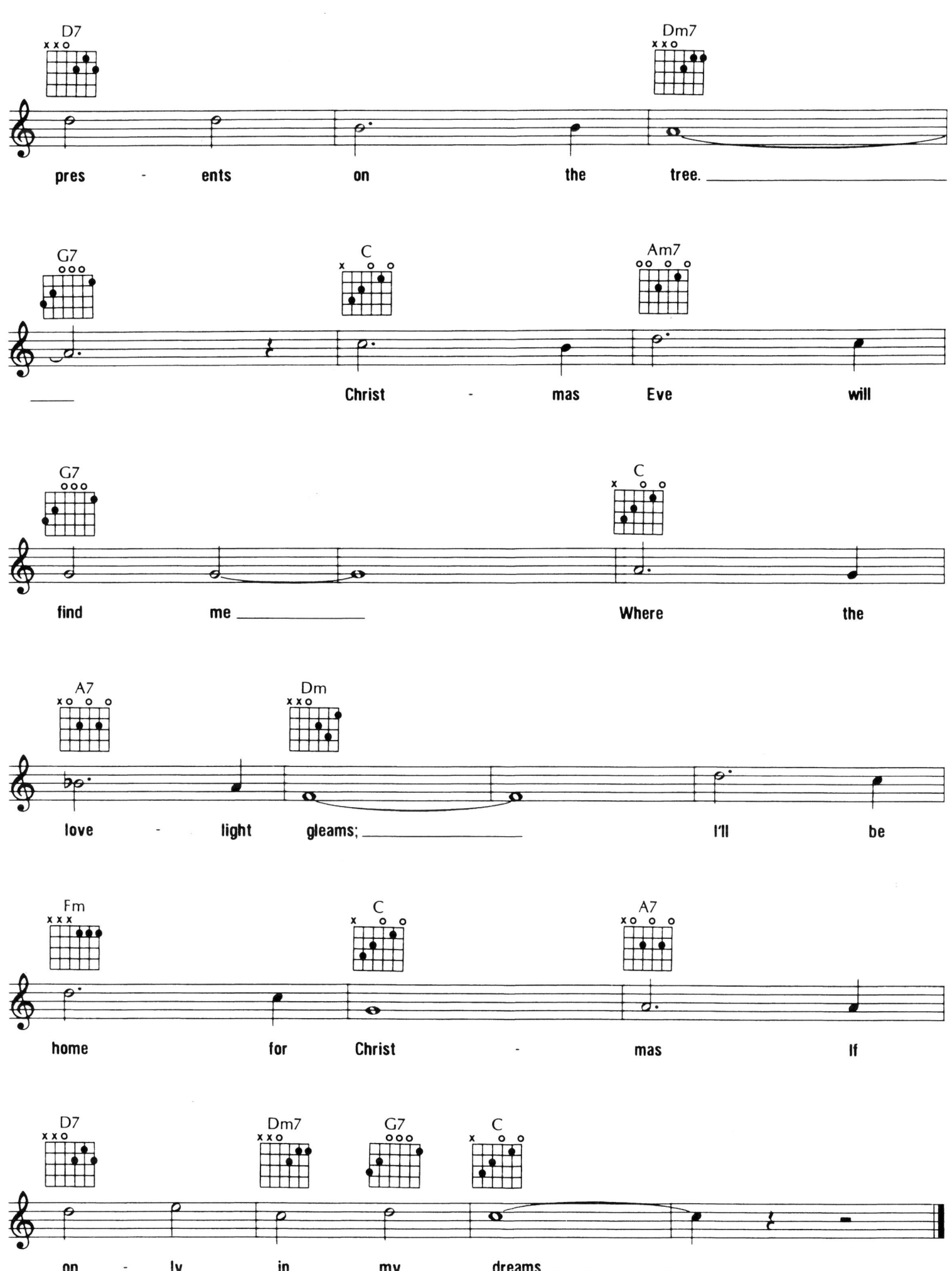

pres - ents on the tree. _____

_____ Christ - mas Eve will

find me _____ Where the

love - light gleams; _____ I'll be

home for Christ - mas If

on - ly in my dreams. _____

LAST CHRISTMAS

Words and Music by
GEORGE MICHAEL

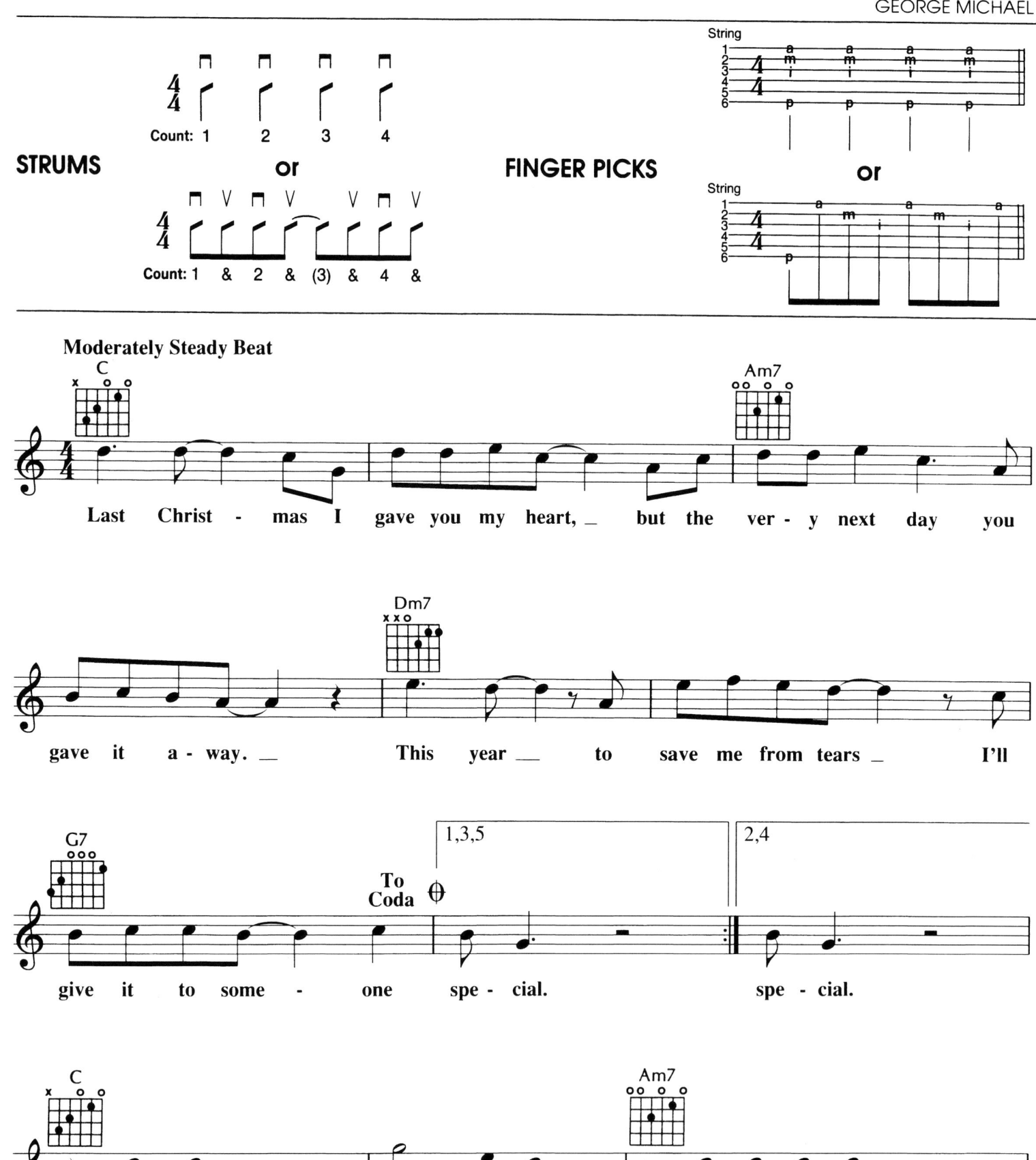

Copyright © 1985 by Morrison-Leahy Music Ltd.
This arrangement Copyright © 1989 by Morrison-Leahy Music Ltd.
Published in the U.S.A. by Chappell & Co.
International Copyright Secured ALL RIGHTS RESERVED Printed in the U.S.A
Unauthorized copying, arranging, adapting, recording or public performance is an infringement of copyright.
Infringers are liable under the law.

you still catch my eye. Tell me ba - by, do you re - cog - nize me?

Well, it's been a year it does - n't sur - prise ___ me.

(Spoken) Hap - py Christ - mas. I wrapped it up and sent it ___ with a note say - ing,

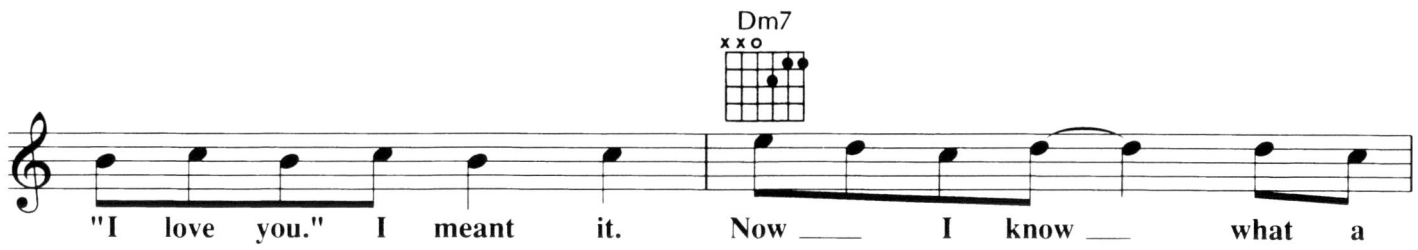
"I love you." I meant it. Now ___ I know ___ what a

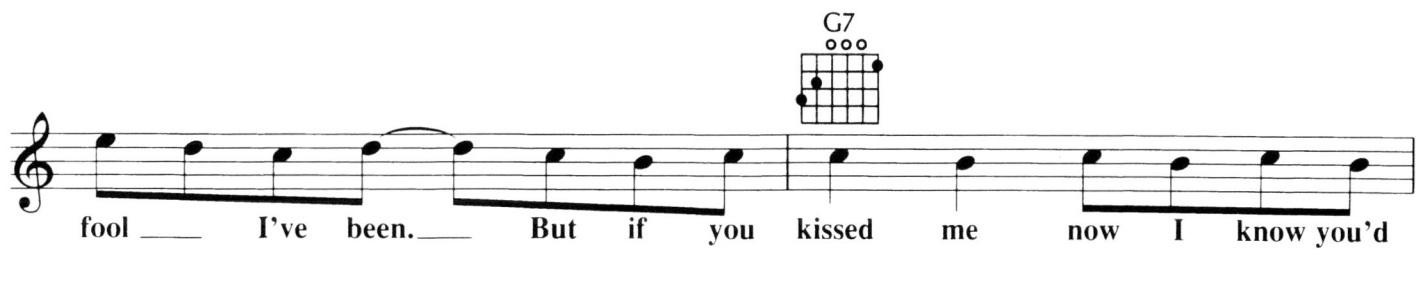
fool ___ I've been.___ But if you kissed me now I know you'd

fool me a - gain. ___   fool me a - gain. ___   spe - cial. ___   A

33

face   on   a   lov - er   with   a   fire   in   his   heart,___   a

man   un - der   cov - er   but   you   tore   him   a - part. __   *(Spoken) May - be   next year*

I'll   give   it   to   some - one,   I'll   give   it   to   some - one   spe -

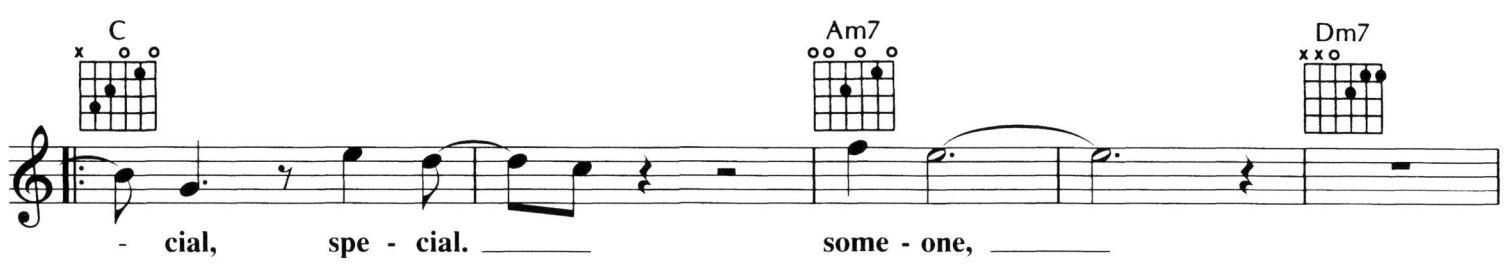

- cial,   spe - cial. _____   some - one, _____

Repeat and Fade

some - one.   I'll   give   it   to   some - one,   I'll   give   it   to   some - one   spe -

Additional Lyrics

2. A crowded room, friends with tired eyes.
   I'm hiding from you and your soul of ice.
   My god, I thought you were someone to re-ly on.
   Me, I guess I was a shoulder to cry on.
   A face on a lover with a fire in his heart,
   A man under cover but you take me apart.
   Oo, now I've found a new love.
   You'll never fool me again.

MERRY, MERRY CHRISTMAS BABY

By MARGO SYLVIA
and GIL LOPEZ

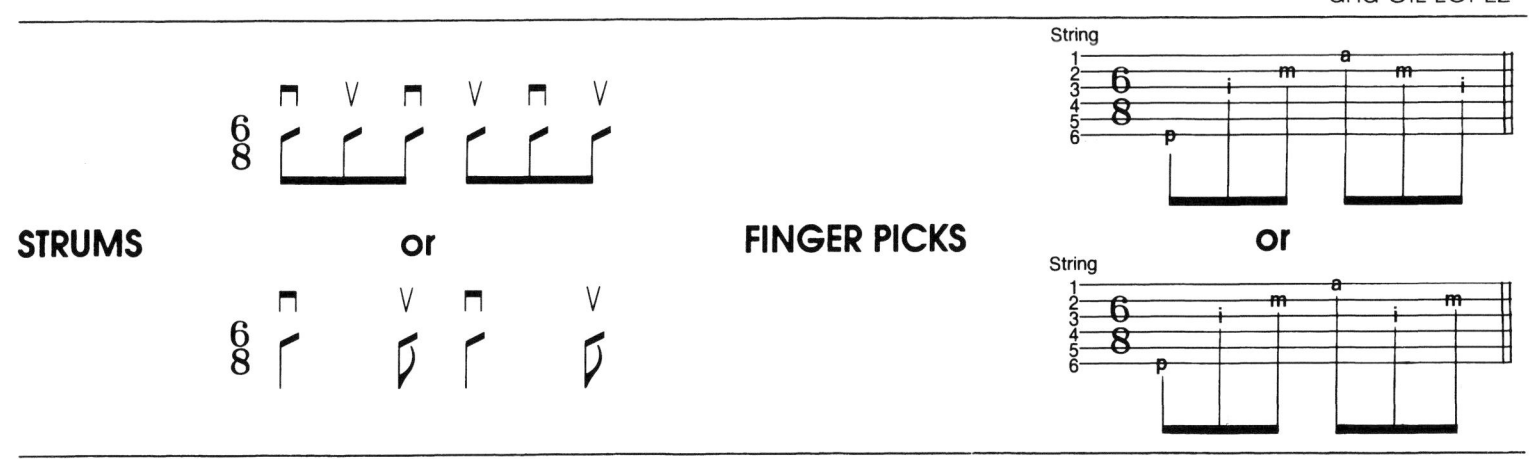

STRUMS or **FINGER PICKS** or

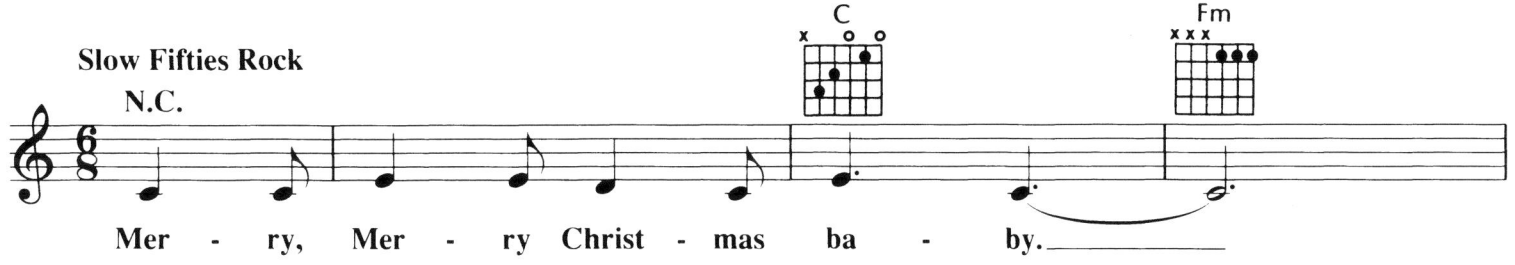

Mer - ry, Mer - ry Christ - mas ba - by.

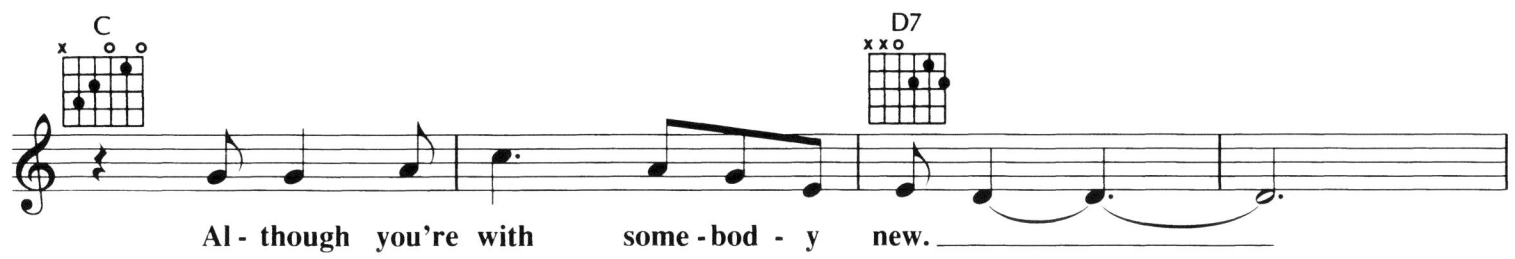

Al - though you're with some -bod - y new.

Thought I'd send a card to say that I wish this hol - i -

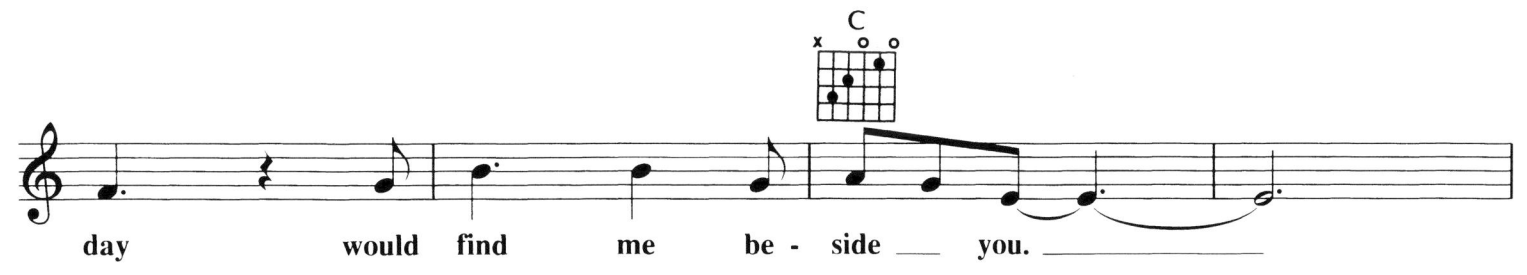

day would find me be - side ___ you.

Copyright © 1956, 1957, 1989 (Renewed) by Arc Music Corp.
All Rights Reserved.

Mer - ry, Mer - ry Christ - mas ba - by. ____

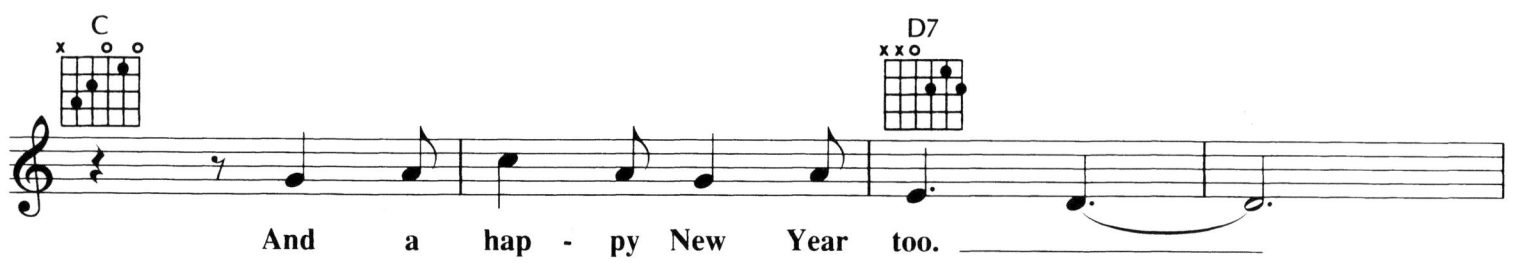

And a hap - py New Year too. ____

It was Christ - mas Eve we met, a hol - i - day I can't for -

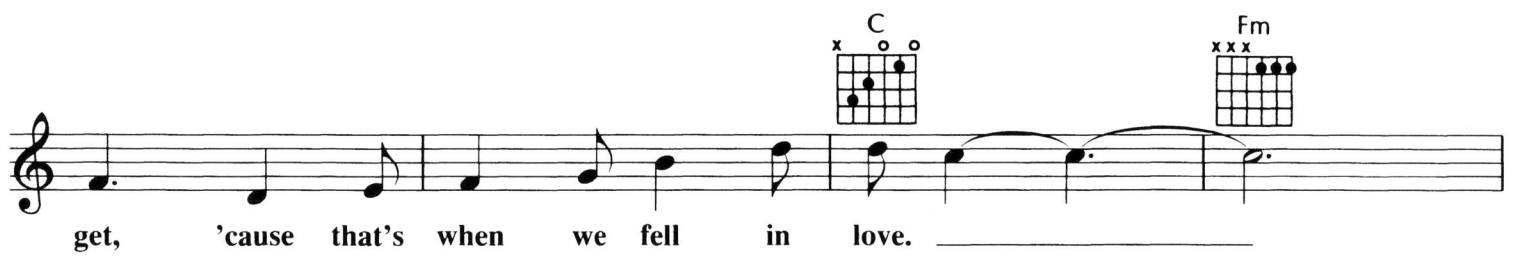

get, 'cause that's when we fell in love. ____

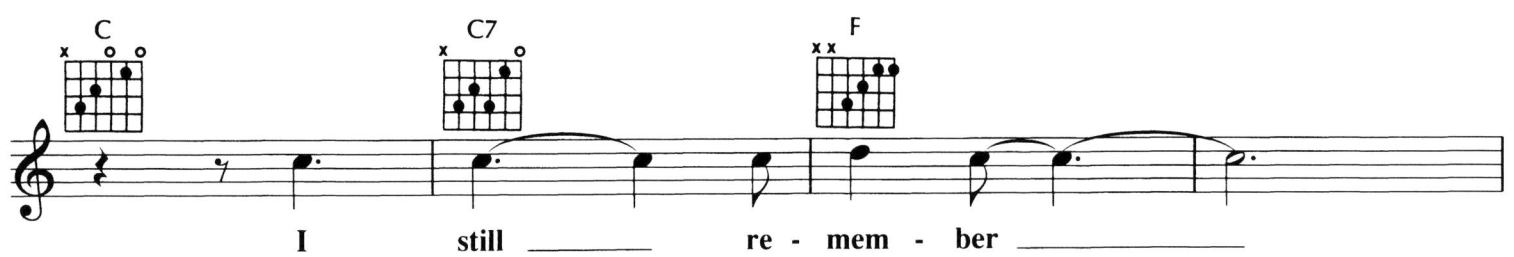

I still ____ re - mem - ber ____

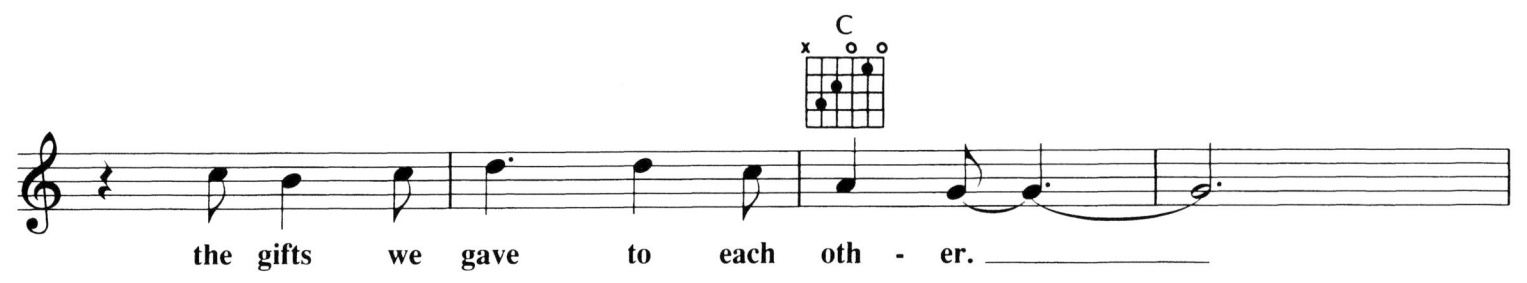

the gifts we gave to each oth - er. ____

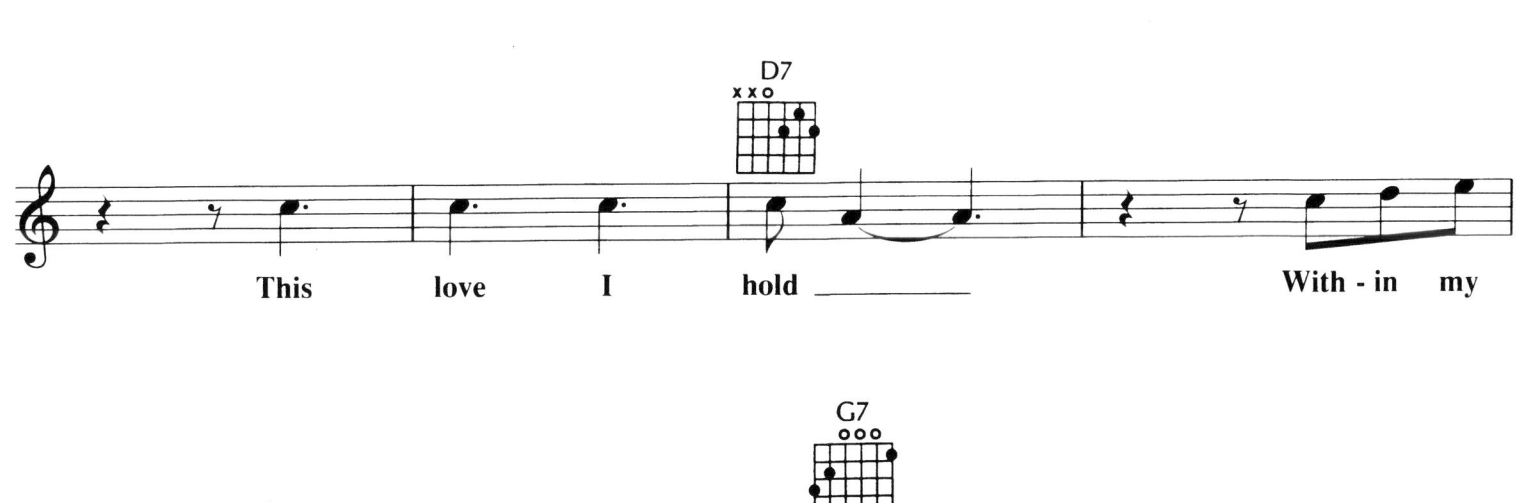

This love   I   hold _____   With - in my

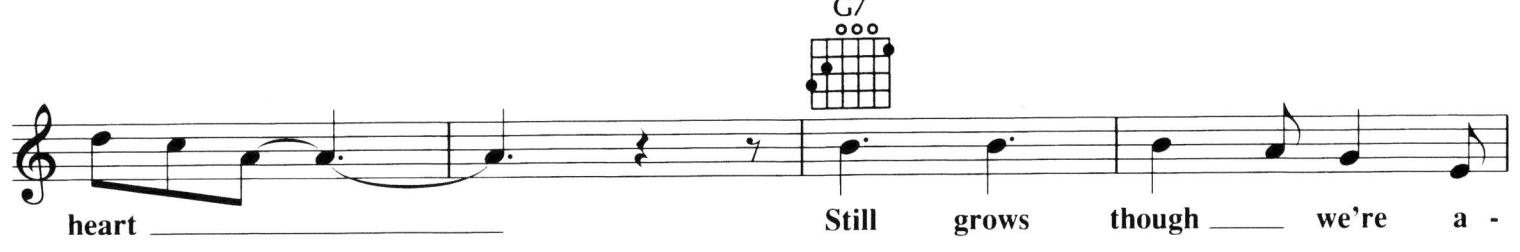

heart _____   Still   grows   though ____   we're a -

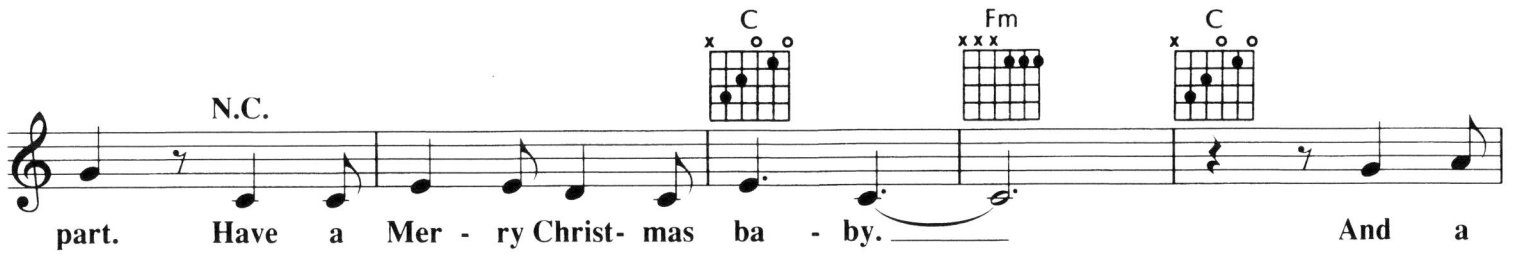

part.   Have   a   Mer - ry Christ - mas   ba - by. _____   And   a

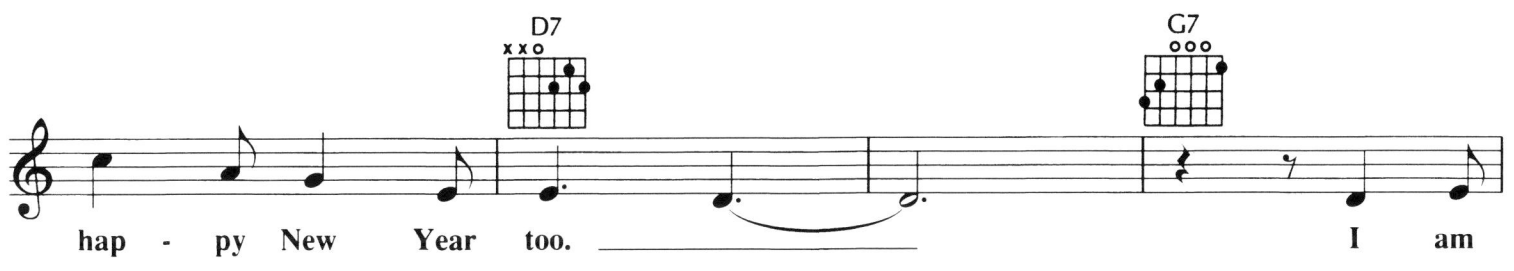

hap - py   New   Year   too. _____   I   am

hop - ing   that   you'll   find   a ____   love   as   true   as   mine   Mer - ry,

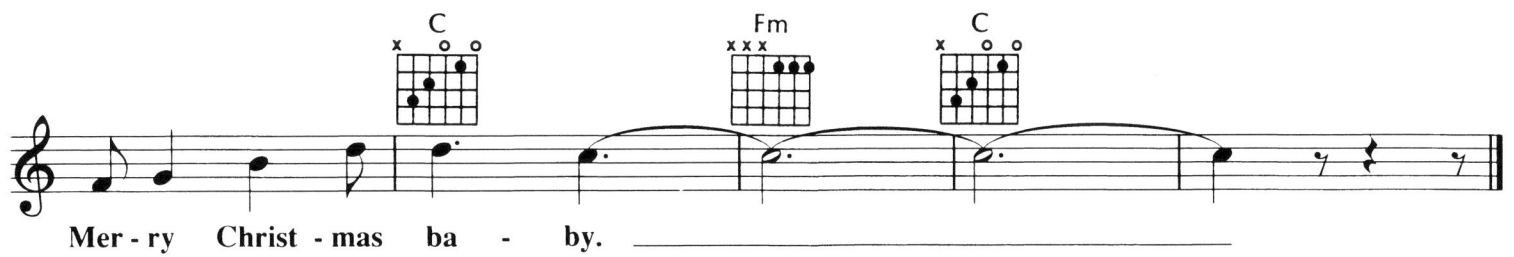

Mer - ry   Christ - mas   ba - by. _____

LET IT SNOW! LET IT SNOW! LET IT SNOW!

Words by SAMMY CAHN
Music by JULE STYNE

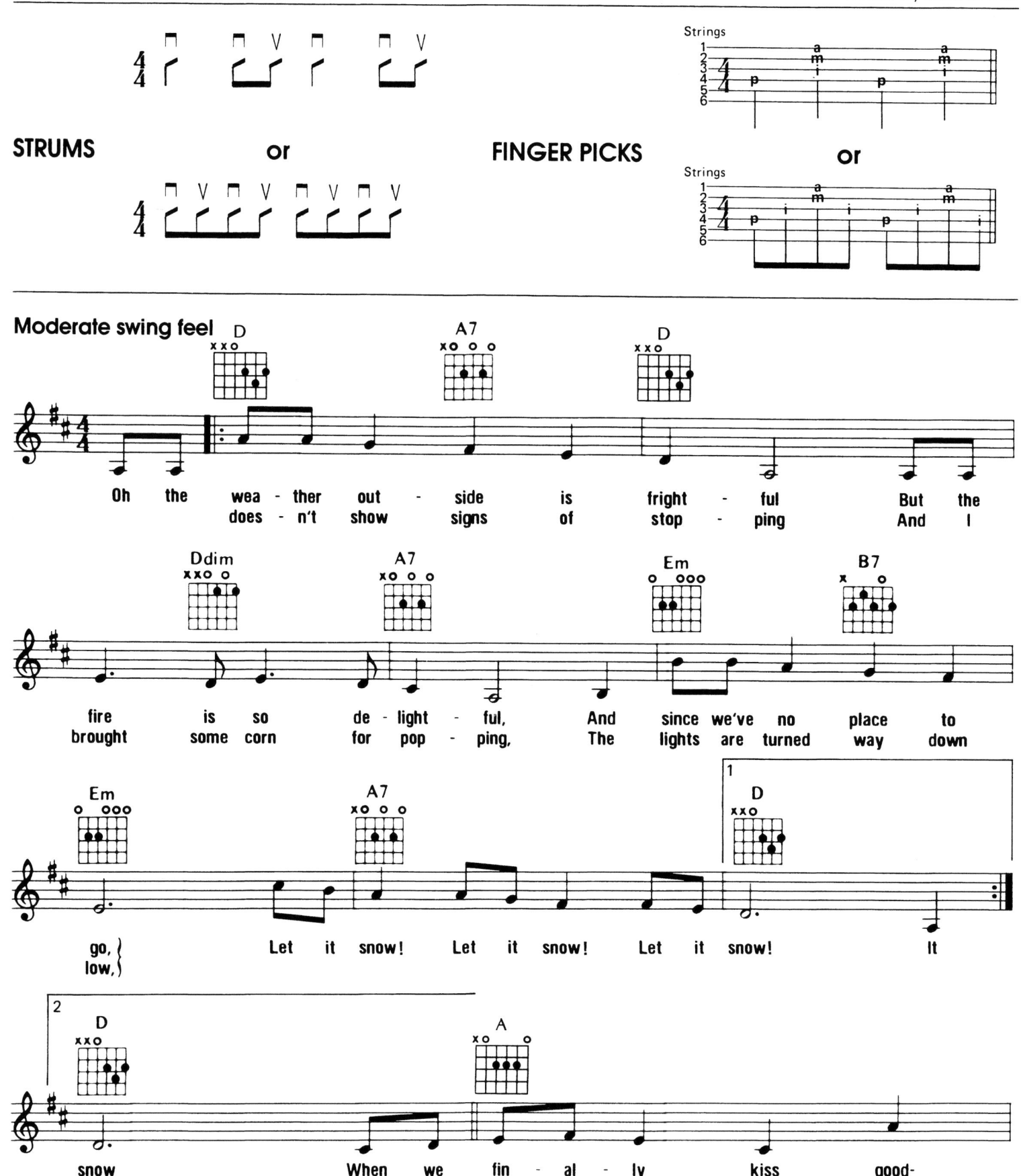

Copyright © 1945 by Jule Styne and Cahn Music, Inc.
Copyright renewed, Styne interest assigned to Producers Music, Inc. (Administered by Chappell & Co.) for the U.S.A. only
This arrangement Copyright © 1989 by Producers Music, Inc. and Cahn Music, Inc.
International Copyright Secured   ALL RIGHTS RESERVED   Printed in the U.S.A.
Unauthorized copying, arranging, adapting, recording or public performance is an infringement of copyright.
Infringers are liable under the law.

THE LITTLE DRUMMER BOY

Words and Music by KATHERINE DAVIS,
HENRY ONORATI and HARRY SIMEONE

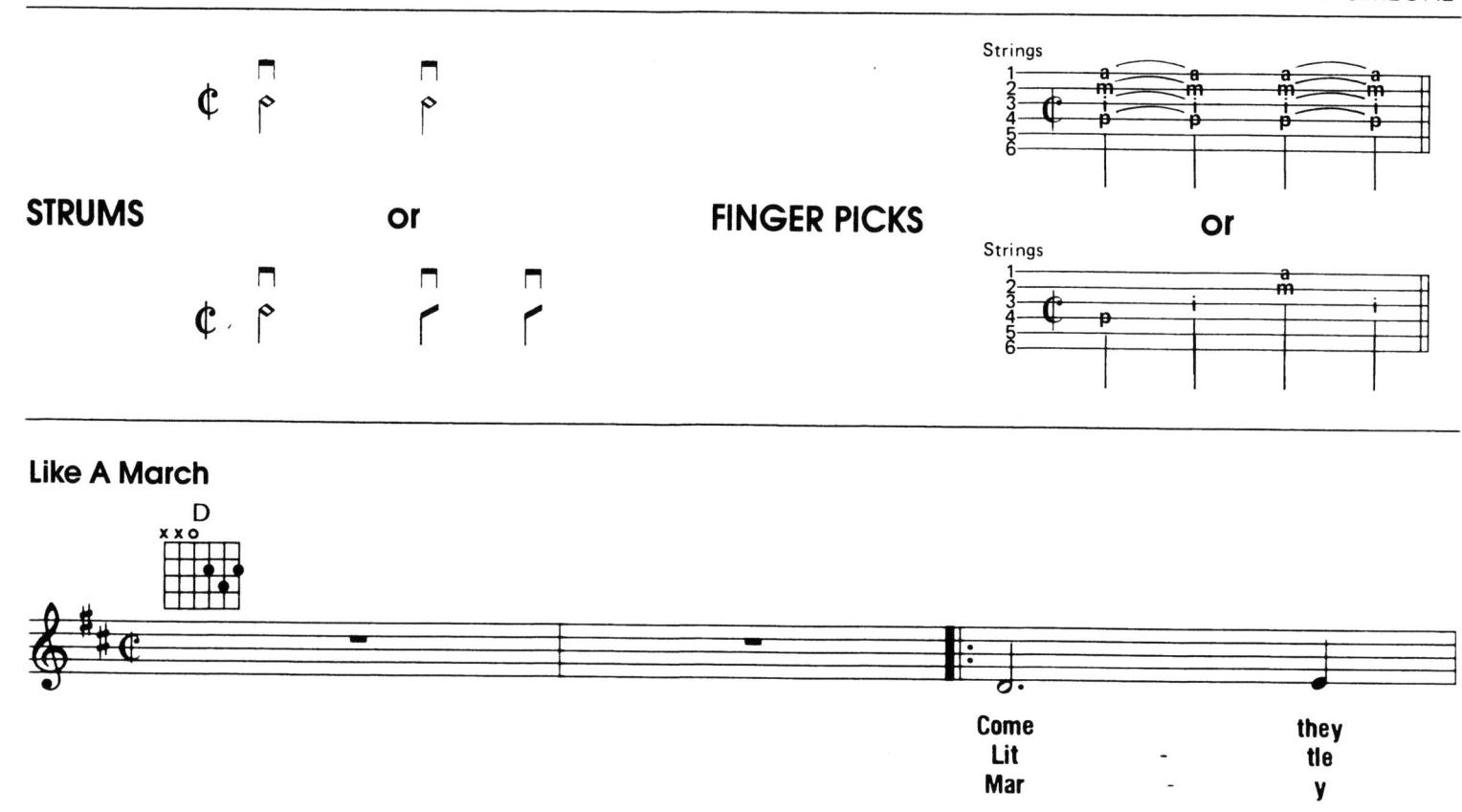

STRUMS   or   FINGER PICKS   or

Like A March

Come ... they
Lit - tle
Mar - y

told me,
Ba - by, } pa - rum pum pum   pum, _____
nod - ded,

A   new   born   King   to   see,
I   am   a   poor   boy   too, } pa-
The   ox   and   lamb   kept   time,

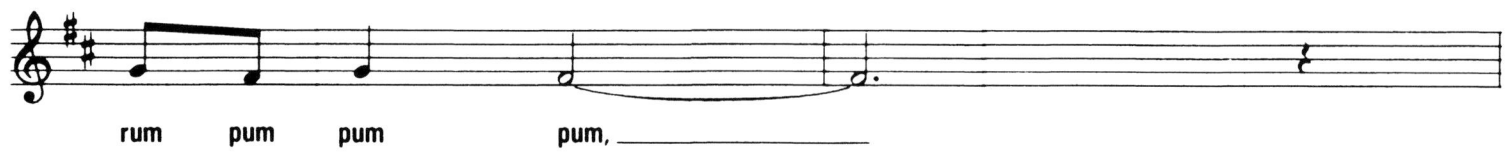

rum   pum   pum   pum, _____

Copyright © 1958, 1989 by Mills Music, Inc. and International Korwin Corp.
Copyright Renewed.
Used with permission. All Rights Reserved.

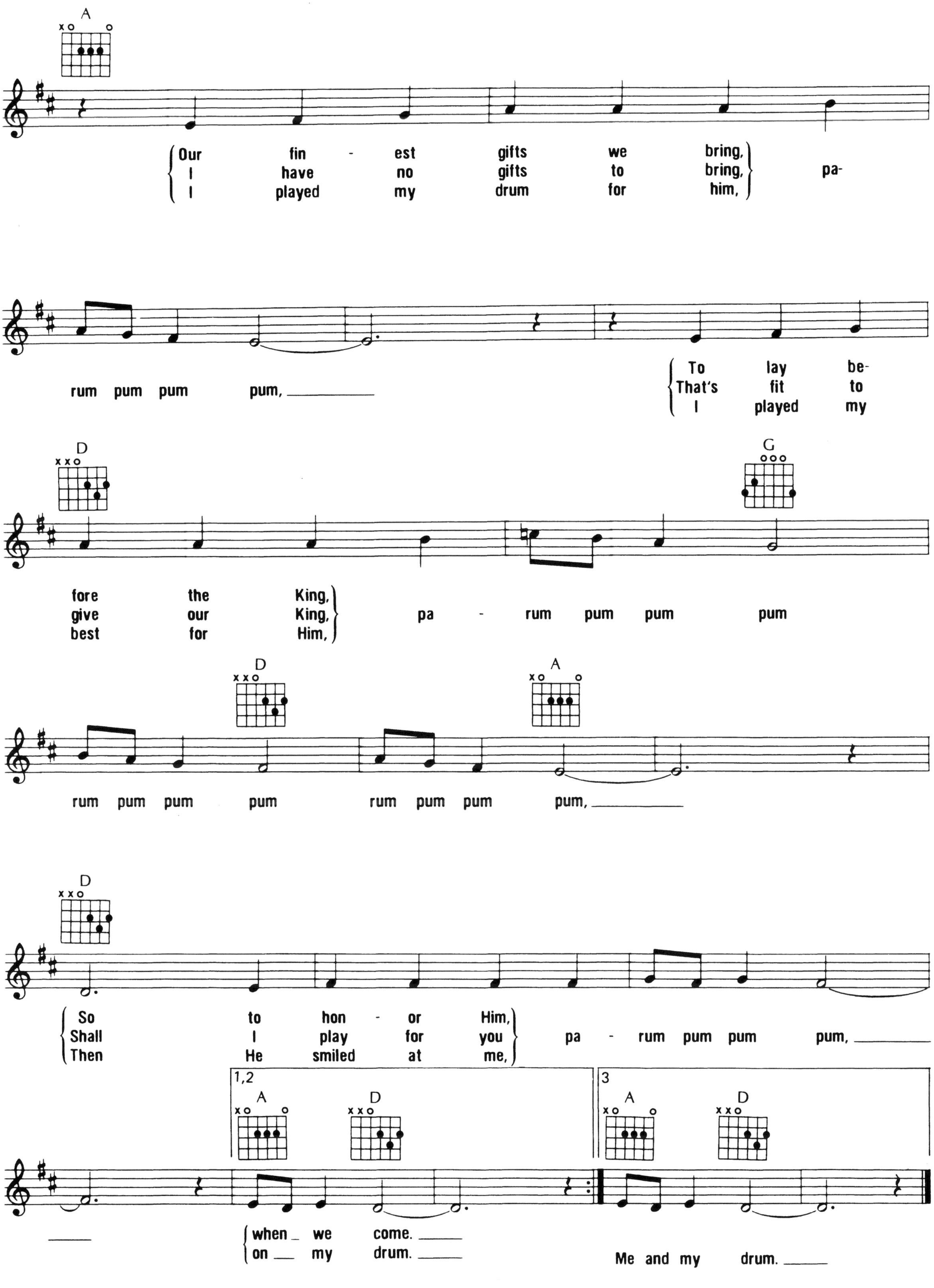

Our fin - est gifts we bring,
I have no gifts to bring,
I played my drum for him,

rum pum pum pum, _____

To lay be-
That's fit to
I played my

fore the King,
give our King,
best for Him,

pa - rum pum pum pum

rum pum pum pum rum pum pum pum, _____

So to hon - or Him,
Shall I play for you
Then He smiled at me,

pa - rum pum pum pum, _____

1,2
when we come. ____
on my drum. ____

3
Me and my drum. ____

41

MY FAVORITE THINGS

(From "THE SOUND OF MUSIC")

Lyrics by OSCAR HAMMERSTEIN II
Music by RICHARD RODGERS

Copyright © 1959 by Richard Rodgers and Oscar Hammerstein II
Copyright Renewed
This arrangement Copyright © 1989 by Richard Rodgers and Oscar Hammerstein II
WILLIAMSON MUSIC, owner of publication and allied rights throughout the Western Hemisphere and Japan.
International Copyright Secured   ALL RIGHTS RESERVED

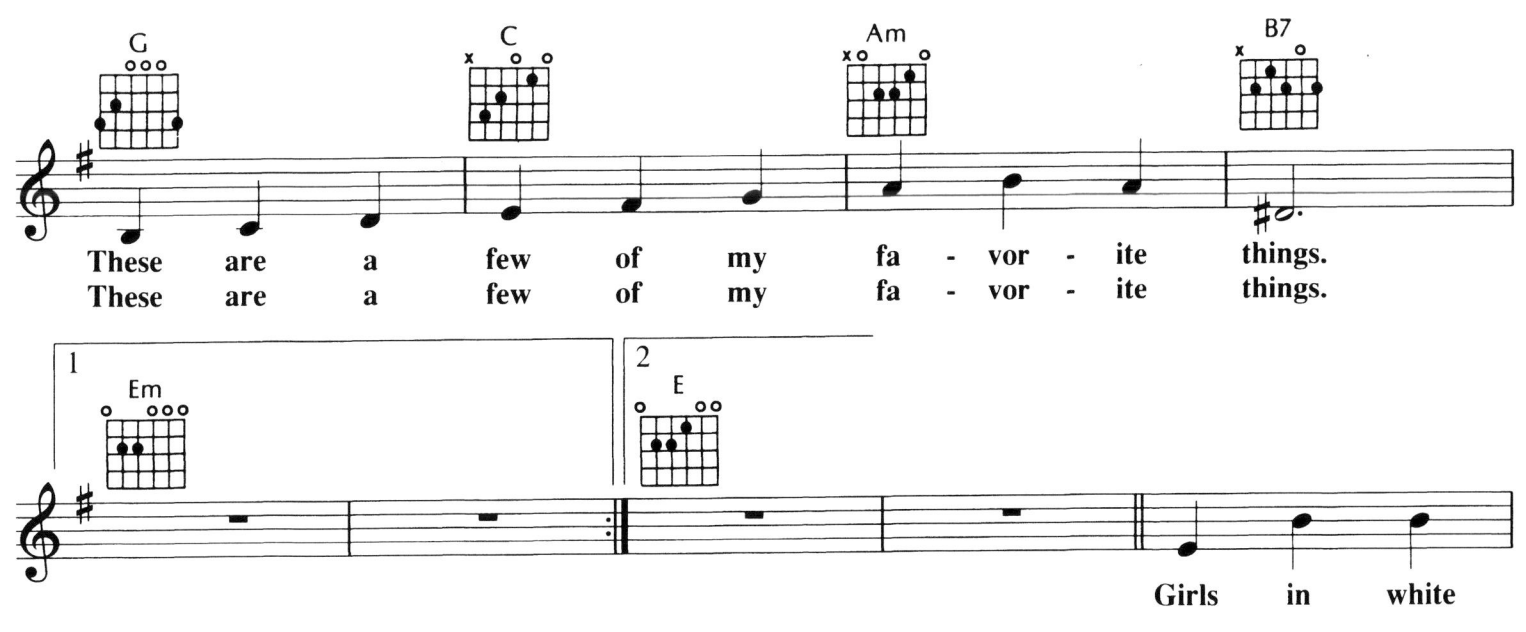

These are a few of my fa - vor - ite things.
These are a few of my fa - vor - ite things.

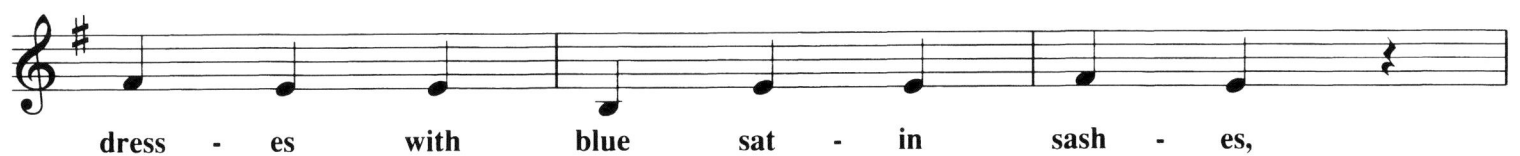

Girls in white

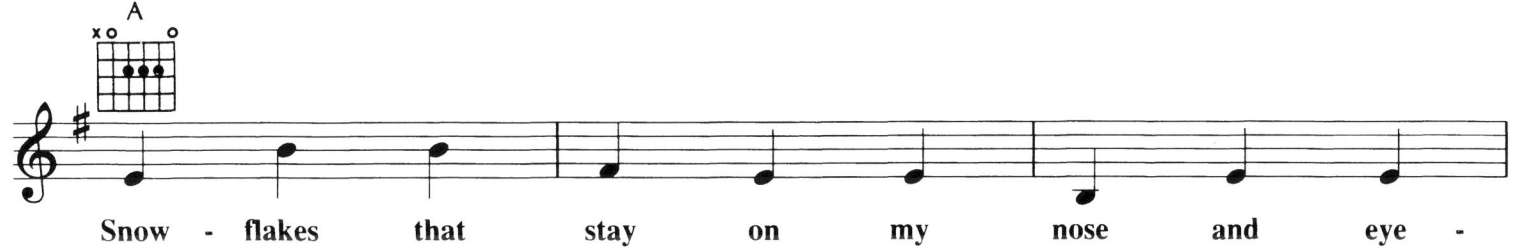

dress - es with blue sat - in sash - es,

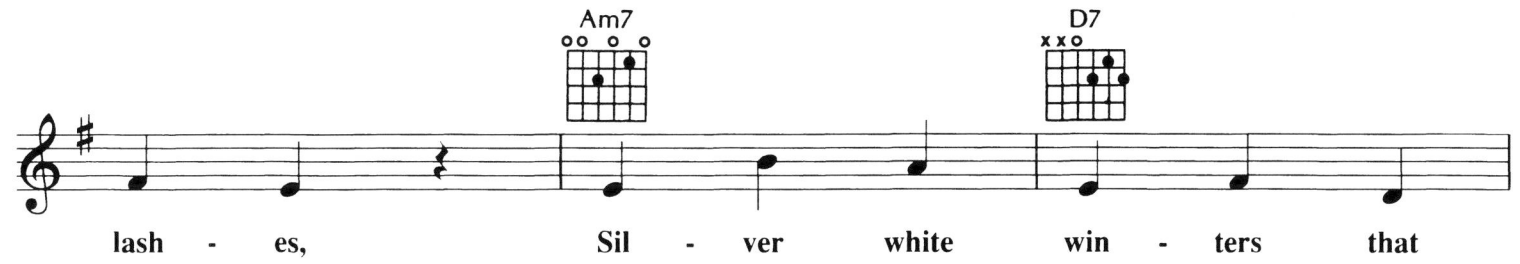

Snow - flakes that stay on my nose and eye -

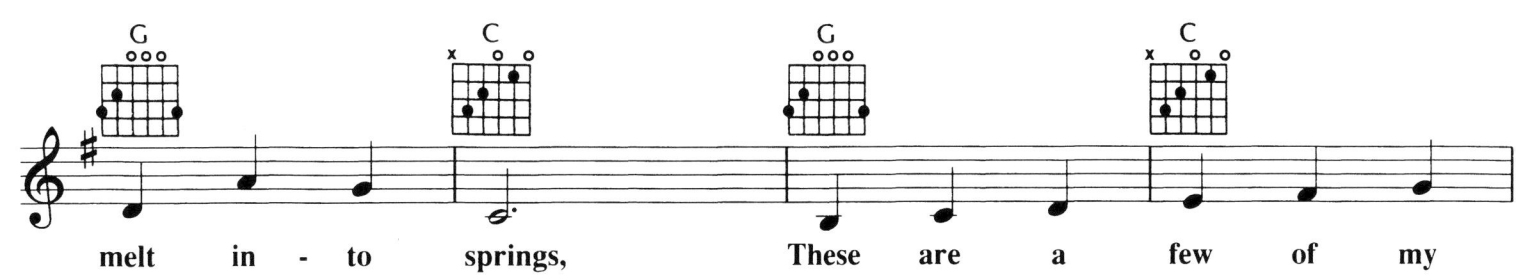

lash - es, Sil - ver white win - ters that

melt in - to springs, These are a few of my

PRETTY PAPER

Words and Music by
WILLIE NELSON

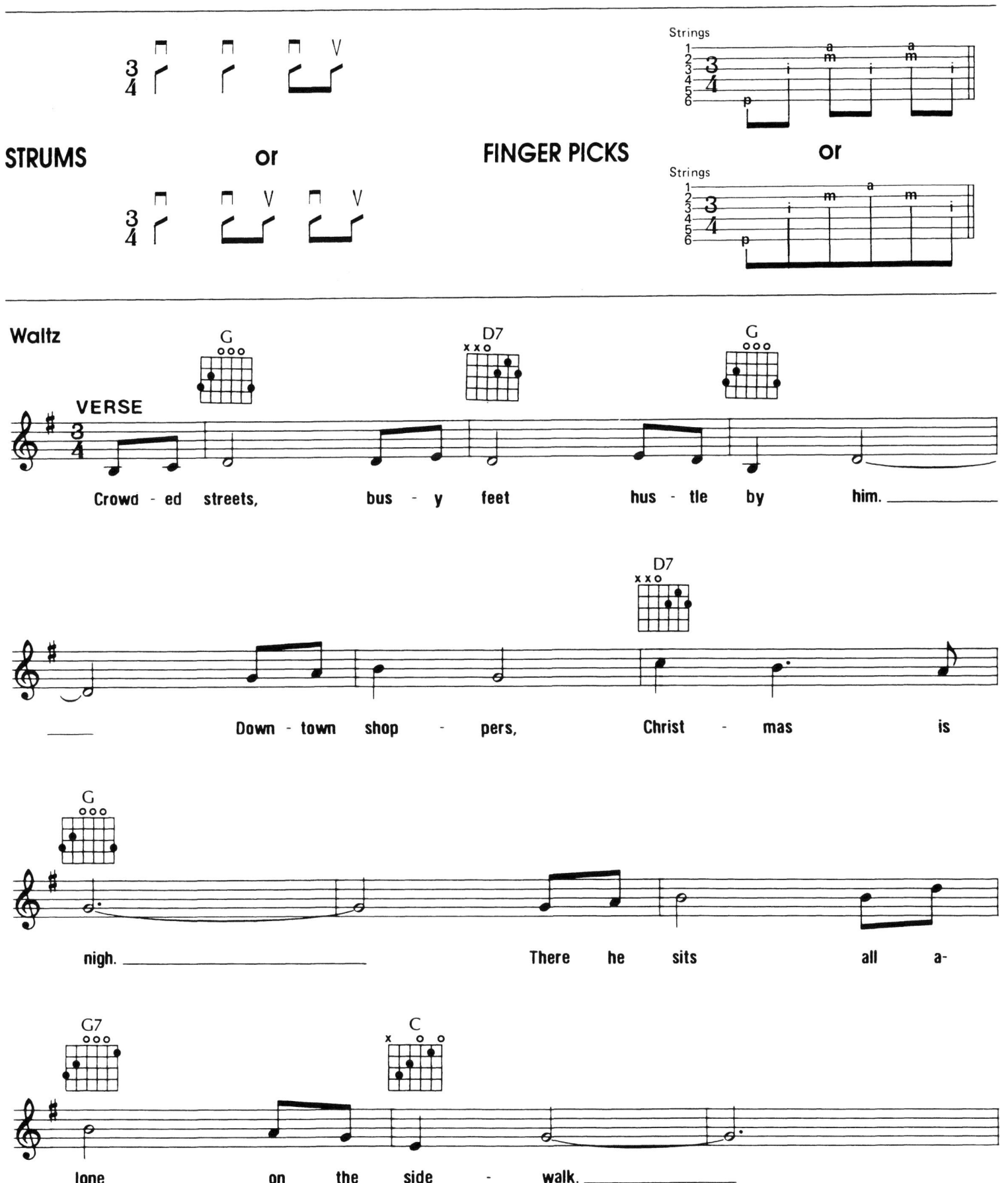

Copyright © 1962 by Tree Publishing Co., Inc., 8 Music Square West, Nashville, TN 37203
This arrangement Copyright © 1989 by Tree Publishing Co., Inc.
International Copyright Secured   Made in U.S.A.   All Rights Reserved

Hop - ing _____ that you won't pass him by. _____

_____ Should you stop; Bet - ter not, much too

bus - y, _____ you're in a hur - ry, my

how time does fly. _____ In the

dis - tance the ring - ing of _____ laugh - ter _____

_____ And in the midst of the laugh - ter he cries. _____

RUDOLPH THE RED-NOSED REINDEER

Music and Lyrics by
JOHNNY MARKS

Freely

Dm7 Em G7 C

You know Dash - er and Dan - cer and Pran - cer and Vix - en,

Dm7 Em G7 C Am E7

Com - et and Cu - pid and Don - ner and Blit - zen. But do you re-

Am Am7 D7 G7

call the most fam - ous rein - deer of all?

C Chords from here **G7**

Moderately Bright

Ru - dolph the Red - nosed Rein - deer   had a ver - y shin - y nose,
All 'of the oth - er rein - deer   used to laugh and call him names,

Copyright © 1949, Renewed 1977 St. Nicholas Music, Inc., 1619 Broadway, New York, New York 10019
This arrangement Copyright © 1989 by St. Nicholas Music, Inc.
All Rights Reserved

49

SANTA CLAUS IS COMING TO TOWN

Words by HAVEN GILLESPIE
Music by J. FRED COOTS

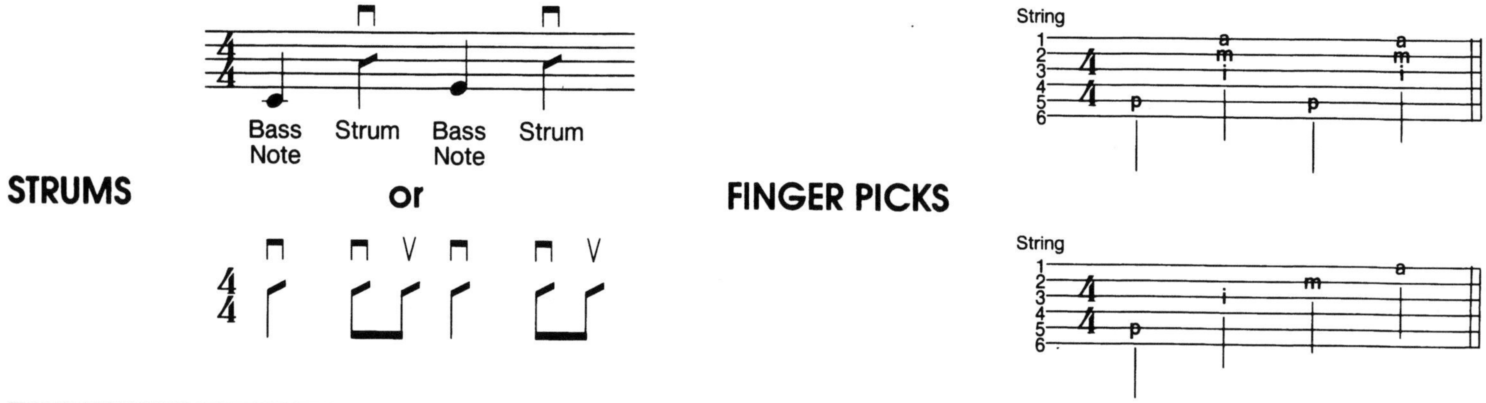
STRUMS
Bass Note
Strum
Bass Note
Strum
or
FINGER PICKS
String
p
i
m
a

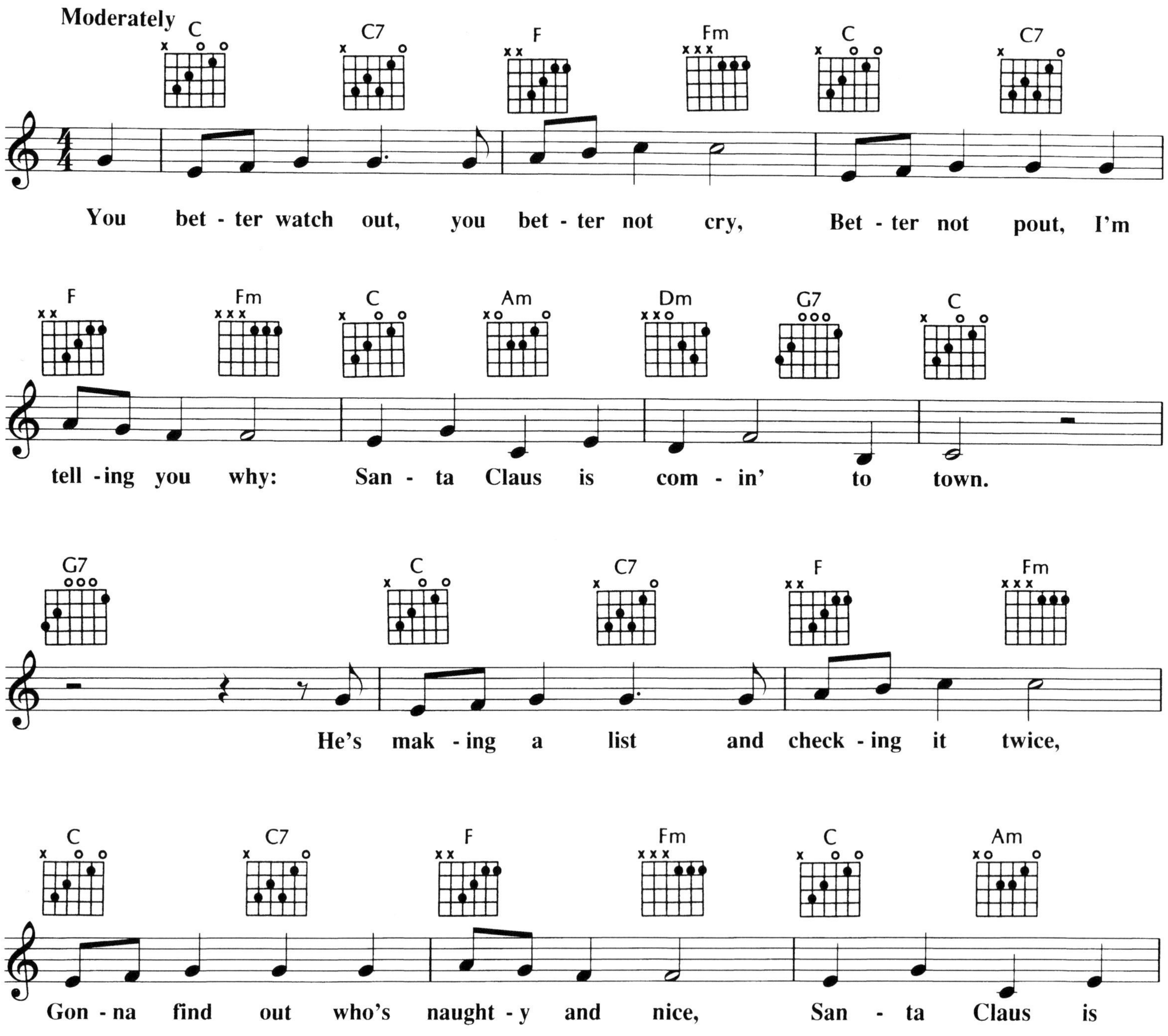
Moderately
C C7 F Fm C C7
You bet - ter watch out, you bet - ter not cry, Bet - ter not pout, I'm
F Fm C Am Dm G7 C
tell - ing you why: San - ta Claus is com - in' to town.
G7 C C7 F Fm
He's mak - ing a list and check - ing it twice,
C C7 F Fm C Am
Gon - na find out who's naught - y and nice, San - ta Claus is

Copyright © 1934 (Renewed 1962), 1989 LEO FEIST, INC.
All Rights of LEO FEIST, INC. Assigned to SBK CATALOGUE PARTNERSHIP
All Rights Controlled and Administered by SBK FEIST CATALOG INC.
International Copyright Secured All Rights Reserved

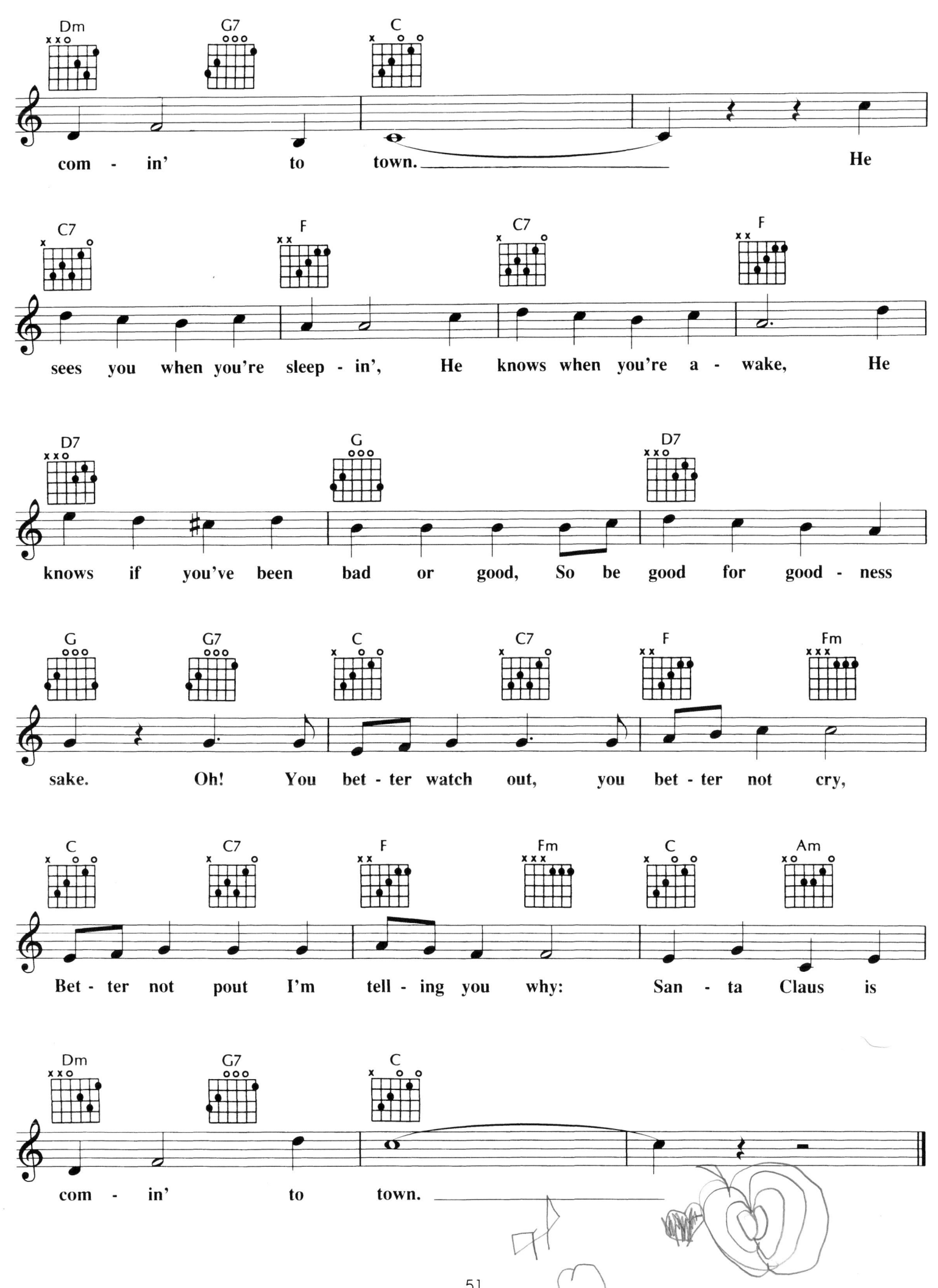

SHAKE ME I RATTLE

(Squeeze Me I Cry)

Words and Music by HAL HACKADY
and CHARLES NAYLOR

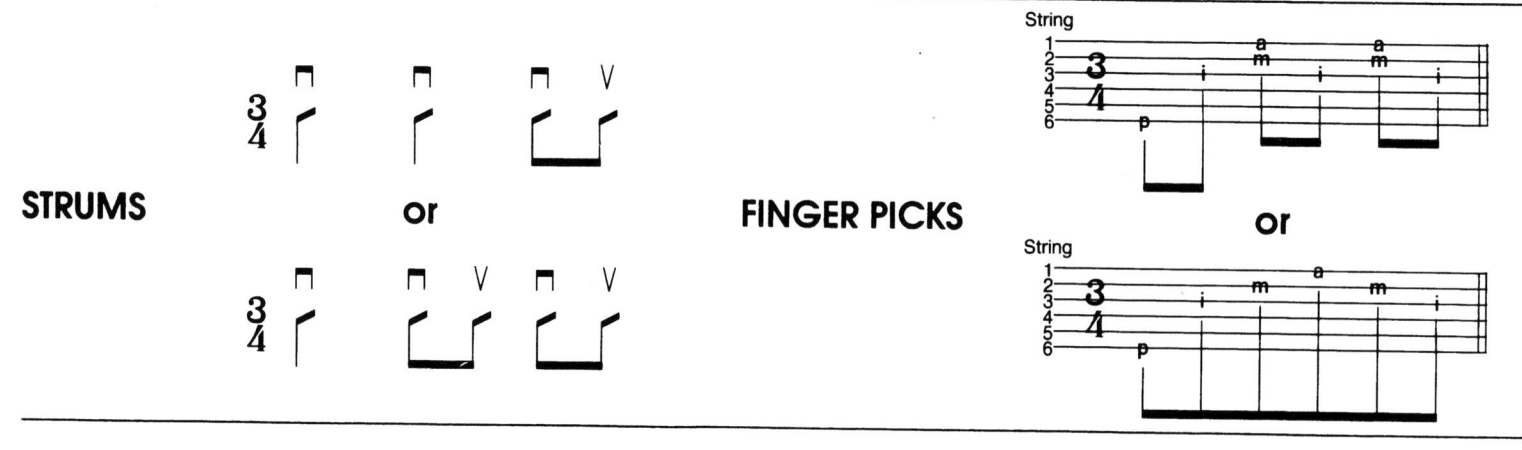

STRUMS   or   FINGER PICKS   or

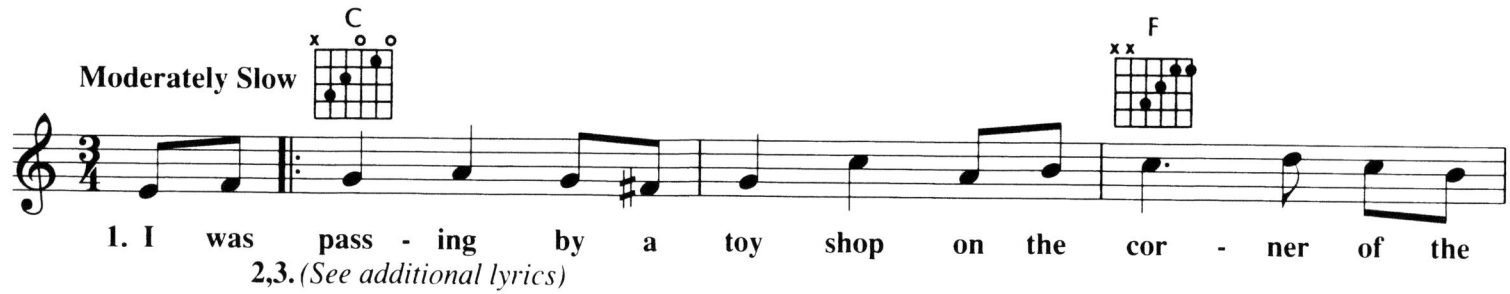

Moderately Slow

1. I was pass - ing by a toy shop on the cor - ner of the

2,3. *(See additional lyrics)*

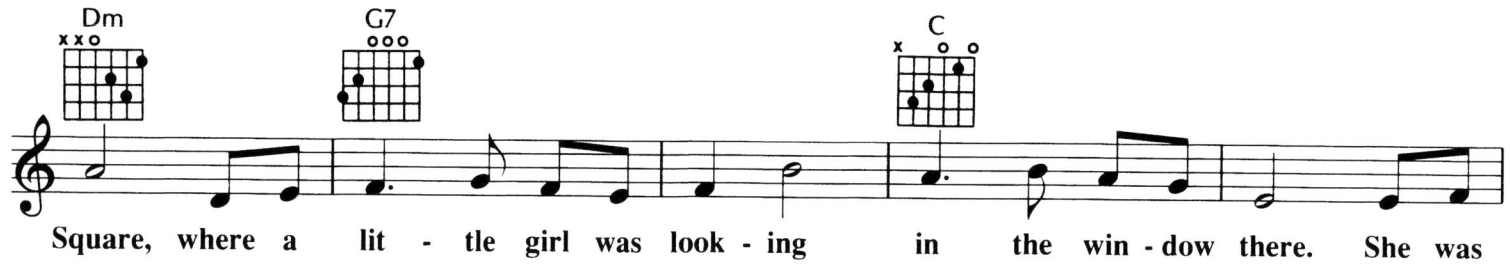

Square, where a lit - tle girl was look - ing in the win - dow there. She was

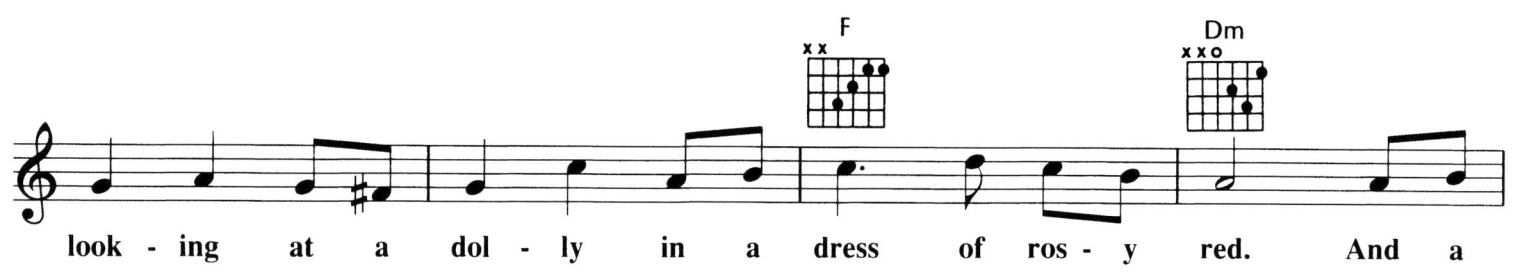

look - ing at a dol - ly in a dress of ros - y red. And a

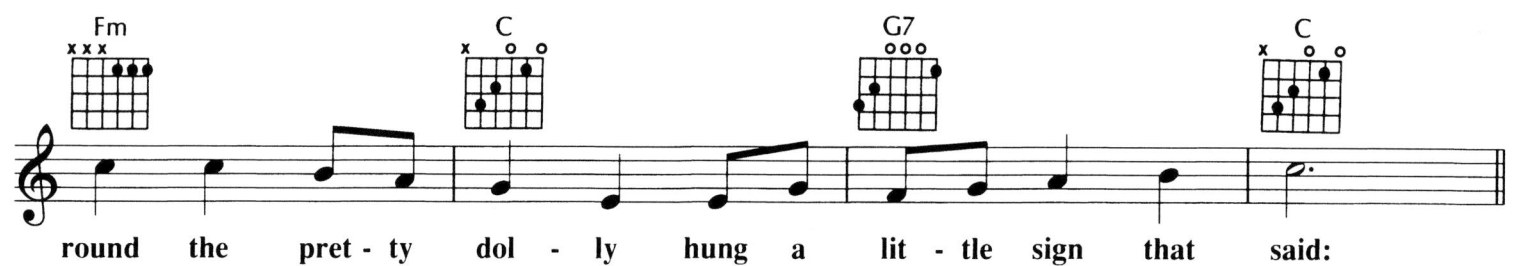

round the pret - ty dol - ly hung a lit - tle sign that said:

Copyright © 1957 (Renewed) by Regent Music Corporation
This arrangement Copyright © 1989 by Regent Music Corporation
All Rights Reserved

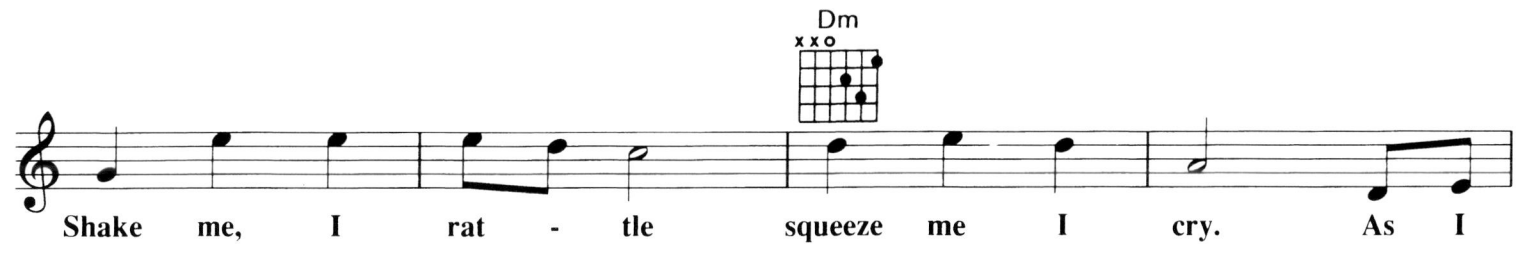

Shake me, I rat - tle squeeze me I cry. As I

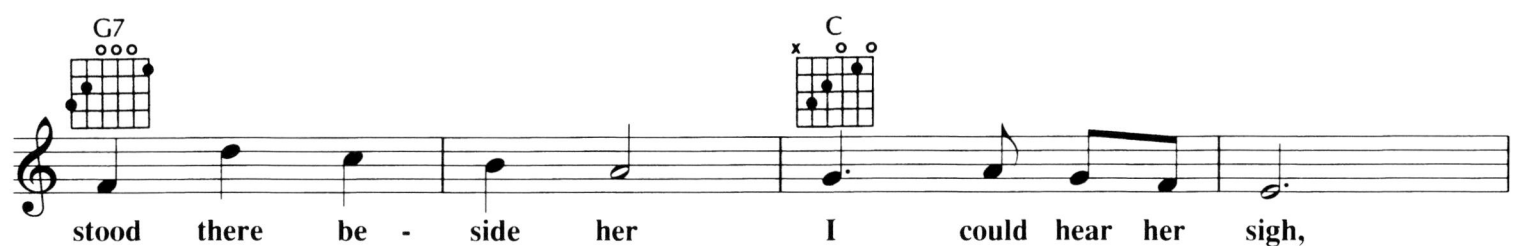

stood there be - side her I could hear her sigh,

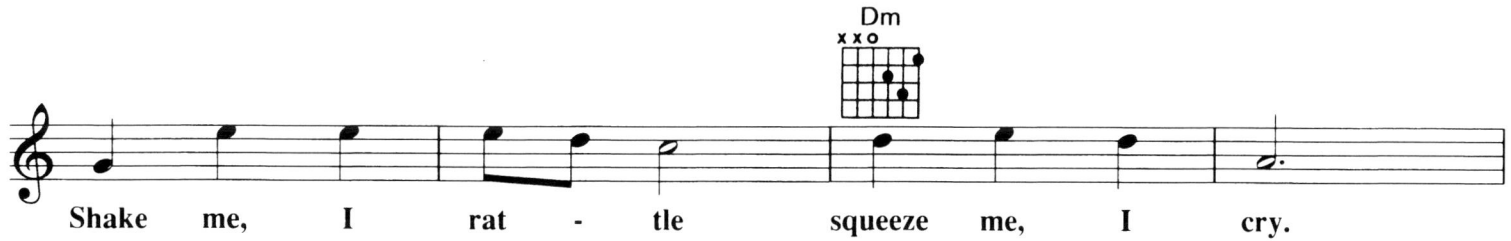

Shake me, I rat - tle squeeze me, I cry.

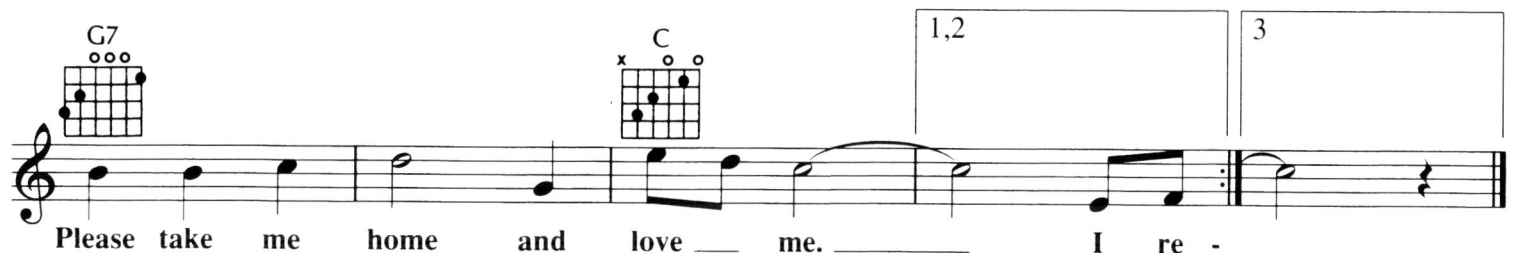

Please take me home and love ___ me. _____ I re -

Additional Lyrics

2. I recalled another toy shop on a square so long ago.
   Where I saw a little dolly that I wanted so.
   I remembered, I remembered how I longed to make it mine
   And around the other dolly hung another little sign:

Chorus   Shake me, I rattle squeeze me, I cry.
         I had counted my pennies, Just a penny shy.
         Shake me I rattle squeeze me, I cry.
         Please take me home and love me.

3. It was late and snow was falling as the shoppers hurried by
   Past the girlie at the window with her little head held high.
   They were closing up the toy shop as I hurried thru the door
   Just in time to buy the dolly that her heart was longing for:

Chorus   Shake me, I rattle squeeze me, I cry.
         And I gave her the dolly that we both had longed to buy.
         Shake me I rattle squeeze me, I cry.
         Please take me home and love me.

SILVER BELLS

Words and Music by JAY LIVINGSTON
and RAY EVANS

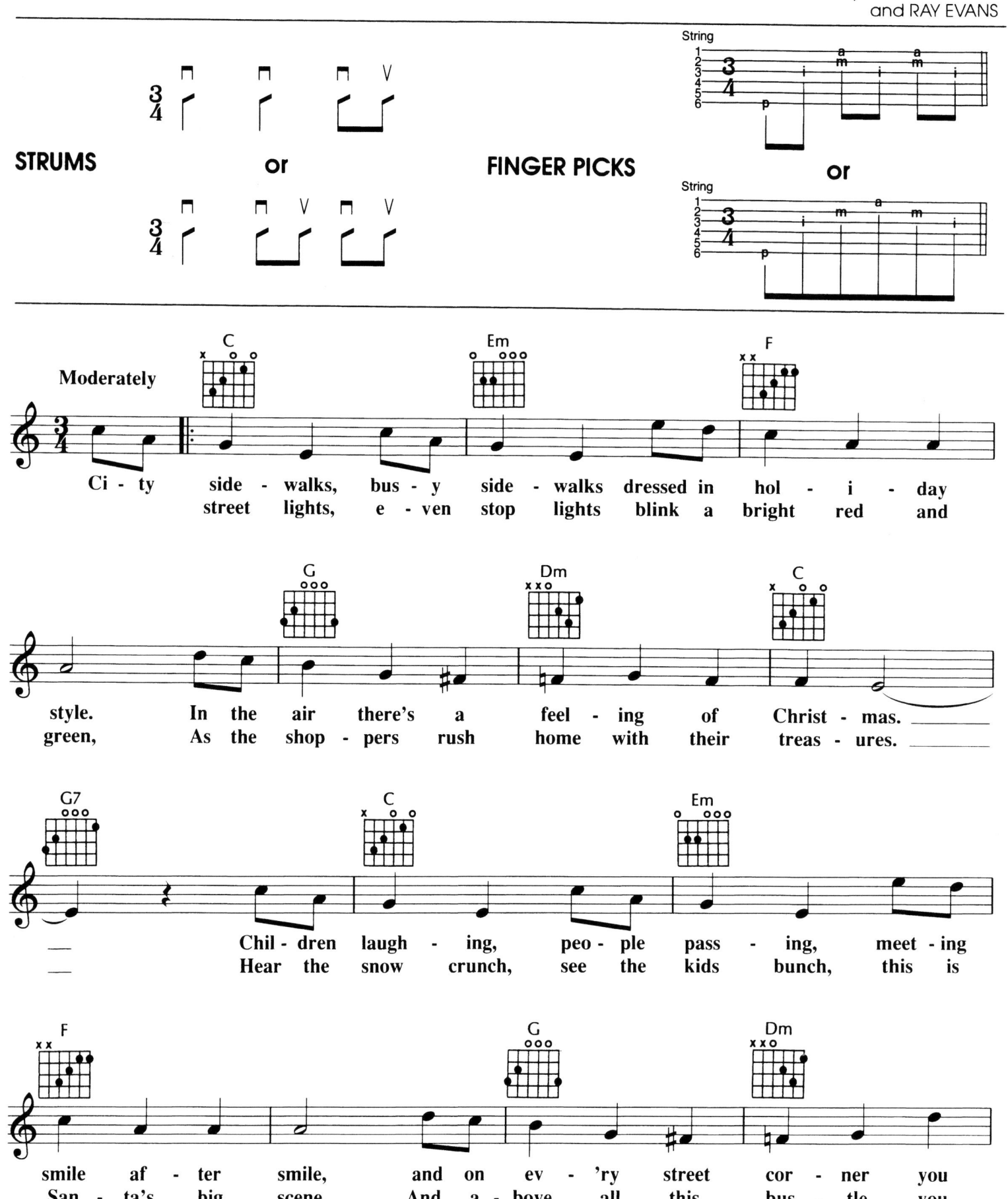

Copyright © 1950, 1989 by Paramount Music Corporation, 1 Gulf & Western Plaza, New York, NY 10023
Copyright Renewed 1977 by Paramount Music Corporation
International Copyright Secured   All Rights Reserved

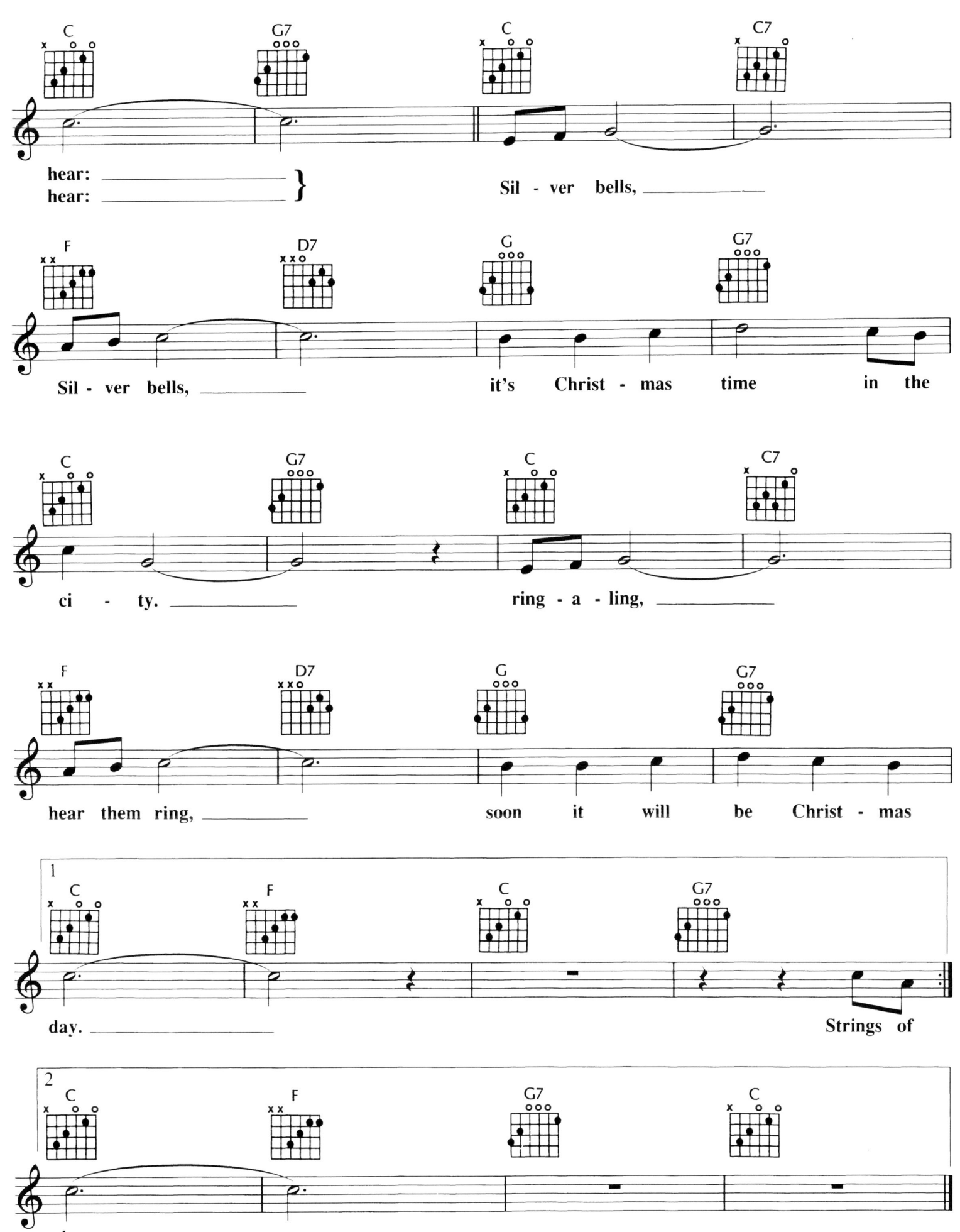

SUZY SNOWFLAKE

Words and Music by SID TEPPER
and ROY BENNETT

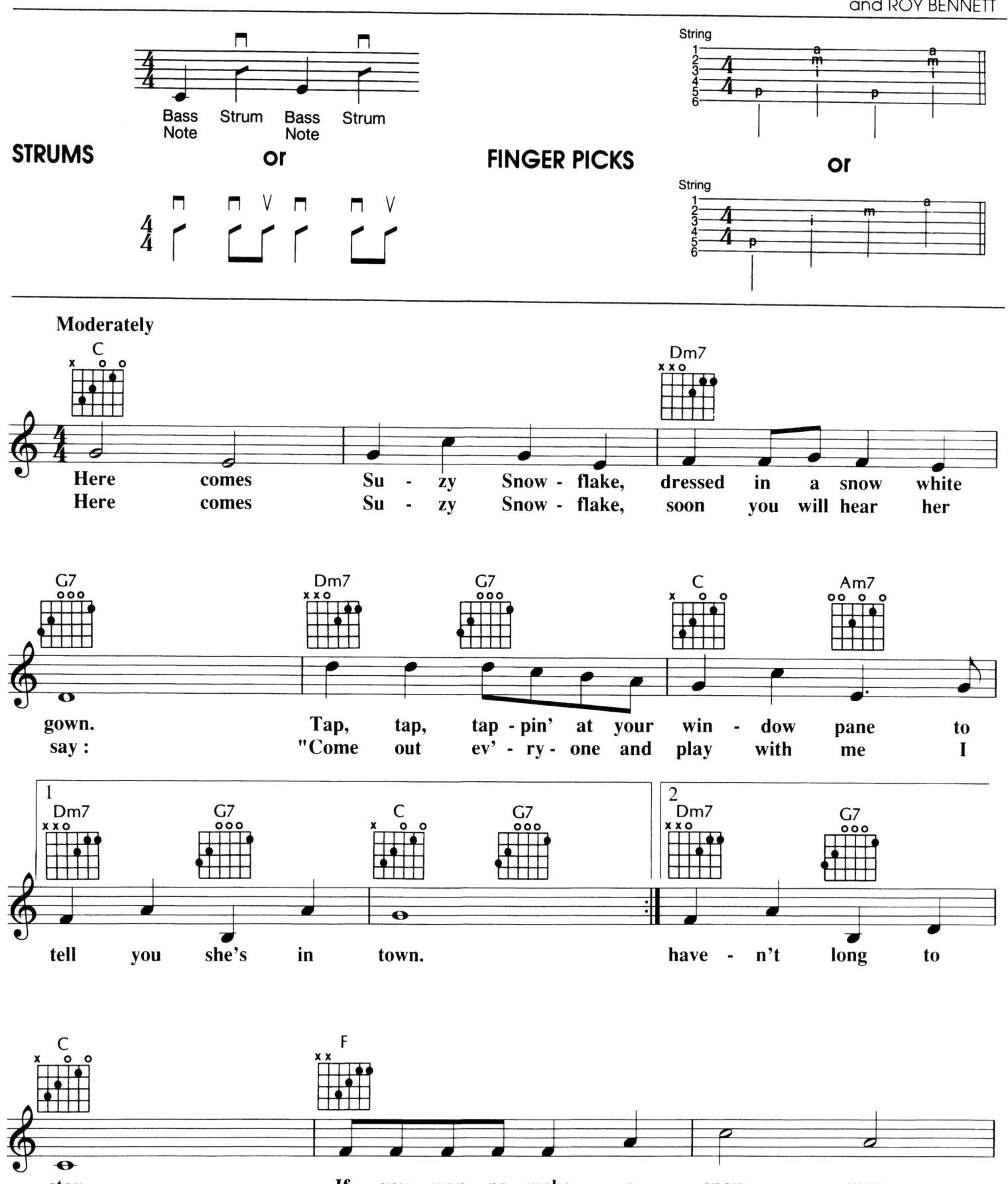

Copyright © 1951 by Alamo Music, Inc.
Copyright Renewed, controlled by Chappell & Co. (Intersong Music, Publisher)
This arrangement Copyright © 1989 by Chappell & Co.
International Copyright Secured   ALL RIGHTS RESERVED   Printed in the U.S.A.
Unauthorized copying, arranging, adapting, recording or public performance is an infringement of copyright.
Infringers are liable under the law.

SLEIGH RIDE

Words by MITCHELL PARISH
Music by LEROY ANDERSON

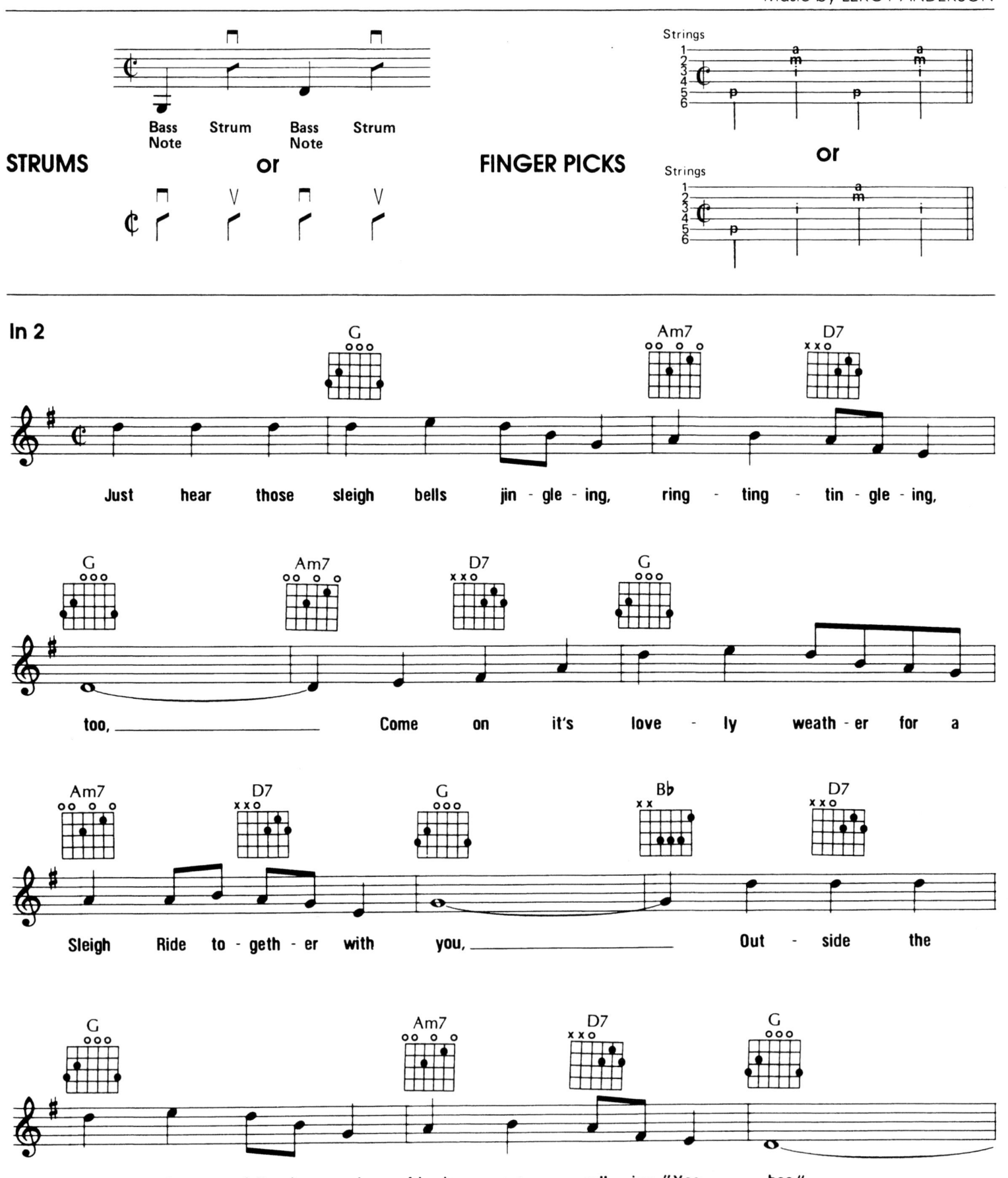

Copyright © 1948, 1950, 1989 by Mills Music, Inc.
c/o Filmtrax Copyright Holdings, Inc.
Copyright Renewed
International Copyright Secured   Made in U.S.A.   All Rights Reserved

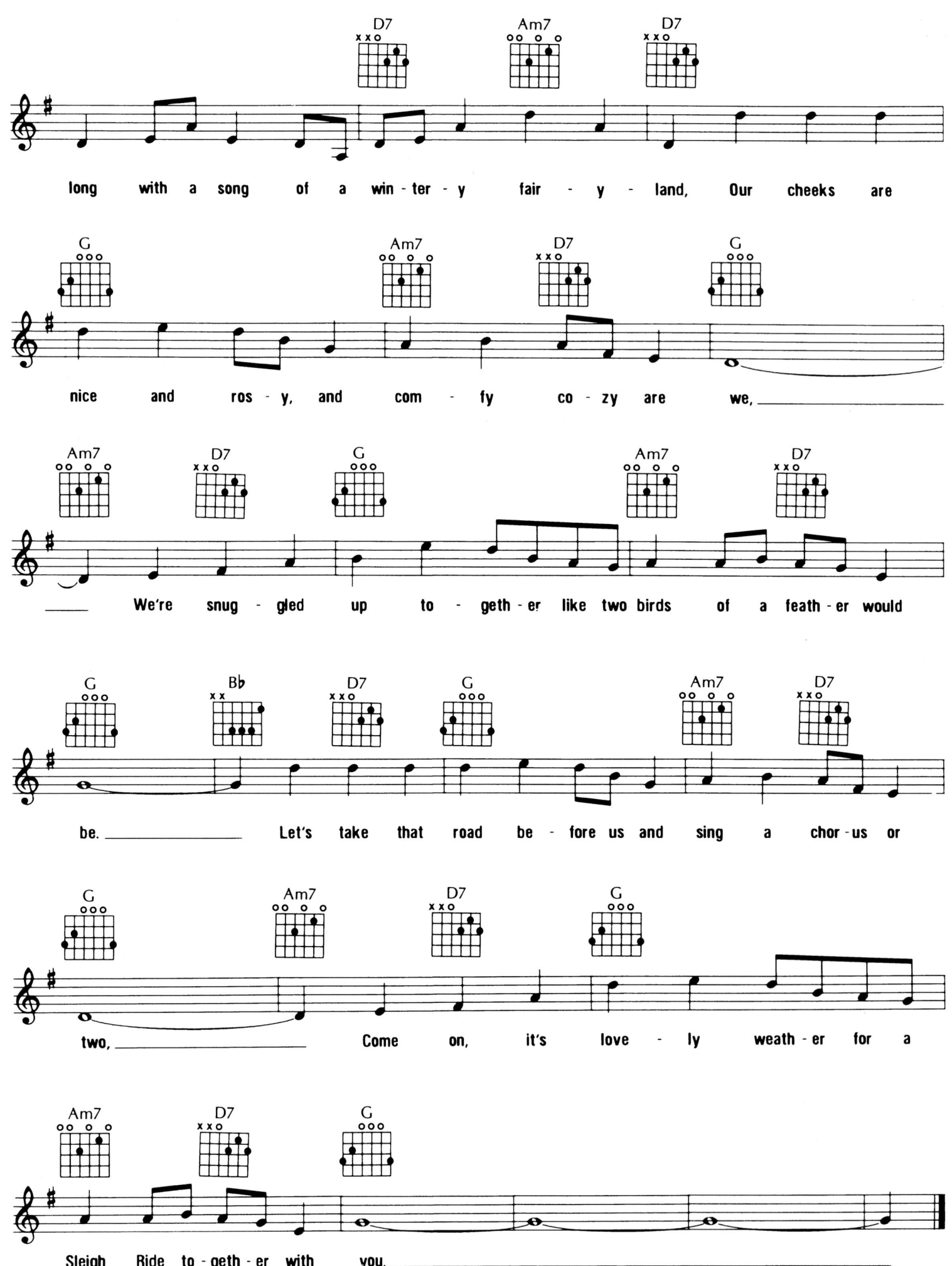

long   with   a   song   of   a   win - ter - y   fair - y - land,   Our   cheeks   are

nice   and   ros - y,   and   com - fy   co - zy   are   we, _____

_____   We're   snug - gled   up   to - geth - er   like   two   birds   of   a   feath - er   would

be. _____   Let's   take   that   road   be - fore   us   and   sing   a   chor - us   or

two, _____   Come   on,   it's   love - ly   weath - er   for   a

Sleigh   Ride   to - geth - er   with   you. _____